As-A-Service

AS A SERVICE

TURN YOUR PRODUCT BASED BUSINESS INTO A SUBSCRIPTION MODEL

YANN TOUTANT

Reviews

"I have known Yann for several years and I can verify that he is the true "As-A-Service" expert".

Urban Odelind, CEO, Foxway Finance AB

"Yann gave great guidance in the initial development of our As-A-Service proposition"

Jeroen Burger, CFO, INNAX

"As an executive and evangelist Yann has been on the forefront of the As-A-Service industry. He has a keen understanding of the business model and walks the talk with Black Winch."

Melle Eijckelhoff, CEO, Alex van Groningen, Sijthoff Media

"Working closely together with Yann is supporting us to set new standards around our As-A-Service ambitions. This is a great opportunity for our customers and partners to leverage".

Erik Swart, Country Leader Enterprise Apple

"Yann is an expert in the world of "As-A-Service" and guided us to improve our performance and business model on our IT and Wi-Fi network so we were able to fulfil our mission: give our visitors an unforgettable experience."

Han Mouton, CFO, Johan Cruijff Arena

Table of Contents

"The Stone Age didn't end because they ran out of stones but as a result of competition from the bronze tools which met people's needs."

Ahmed Zaki Yamani

Foreword by Joseph Pulicano - Accenture

Managing Director Accenture Specialty Finance practice

Can I leave it to someone else to generate the electricity I need?

This question would have been quite puzzling some decades ago. Businesses used to own their power generators, and had to take care of maintenance, services and insurance to protect the resources needed to produce their electricity in-house. Nowadays both businesses and individuals prefer to "use" electricity instead of producing it themselves. Energy is the first market sector which evolved towards a utility model.

The reason is quite obvious: we are buying a service that is complex to produce and deliver. We do not have to manage the equipment needed to produce the energy, since the service provider owns the equipment and keeps it running at all times. On top of the above, flexibility is key! We can easily opt in and up or downgrade the service. Additionally, we can opt out of the service simply and at short notice. And one last thing; the amount we pay is directly correlated to our consumption of the service.

I often mention that service-based offers are indeed not new. However, the sectors where this type of consumption model applies are expanding rapidly, so called 'As-A-Service' offers. As a Managing Director in Accenture's Specialty Finance practice, I help Equipment Finance, Auto Finance and Product companies develop their future strategies and acquire or enhance new digital capabilities. Every morning when browsing the web, I witness that the shift to As-A-Service is the result of a profound change in customer expectations and preferences: society and markets have ignited the transition to servitization on a large scale! This transition operates in a two-fold way: either it is the transition of already long-lasting leasing models to subscription models, or it is simply starting from scratch.

So let me summarize the drivers of this transition by listing the following benefits that today's clients are looking for:

1. Flexibility

Customers expect a high degree of flexibility to meet the variable needs in their own businesses or lives. Seasonality, market uncertainties, and opportunities to address a new market as fast as possible are the driving forces to sign an As-A-Service contract. Unfortunately, the usual leasing fixed payment or fixed term offers available in the market are often not flexible enough to meet the expectations of today's customers.

2. Convenience

End users and resellers / dealers expect fast credit decisions, short turnaround times, reliable billing and efficient customer service. Who wants to wait nowadays? Instant decisions and information based on digital tools are the minimum expectation of customers. This is especially true for Generation Y and Z, being the new type of employees coming into the workplace, as well as becoming active consumers with growing purchasing power.

3. One-stop shopping

As-A-Service is a complete experience that includes all the services needed by the user, provided by one player. Equipment, insurance, maintenance and all ancillary services are bundled together. This requires seamless integration with third-party vendors to provide a single point of entry for the end user while managing the performance risk of each player in the ecosystem.

4. Variability

Customers only expect to pay for what they use. Should I pay a fixed fee to get water from the tap at home? For instance, a price-per-mile offering meets a growing demand from car drivers in search of mobility solutions and not a car. This has been the case for decades in the copier industry, which has been offering price-per-page solutions for a while. Why not in other industries?

5. Multi-channel interaction

Customers interact with their suppliers through a variety of channels, and this increasingly means availability of digital platforms that are easy to use. Users expect those tools to be self-serviced and to provide all the necessary information as well as the ability to transact anytime, anywhere. All services accessible and manageable at their fingertips, from a plane, a meeting room or from the comfort of their homes.

6. Easy Opt-Out

As users, we expect to be able to opt in or out of a service easily and with minimal notice. We also expect a seamless end-of-use experience, which can be made possible by good coordination between the parties involved in end-of-use processes, especially when a device involves reversed logistics operations at the opt out moment. I have other ambitions for my weekends than managing logistics-related matters.

I have read many consistent studies and statistics published over the past decade that have shown a clear shift from ownership to usership for the obvious reasons listed above. This is happening across many industries, both B2C and B2B related. Ownership of an asset is no longer seen as a priority over use, across a growing range of asset classes, every day!

Another glaring example that applies to an increasing number of people living in large cities is the fact that car owners are becoming a minority in urban areas. These days, more people use a combination of alternative means of transport, like public transport, car rental, or car sharing services in order to meet the mobility needs they have at a certain moment. In a few years, when autonomous vehicles become a reality, car owners will become an "endangered species" and we will mostly be signing up to car subscription services.

A new Industrial Revolution?

Are we entering into a new industrial revolution? The trend towards As-A-Service is turning into the new way of doing business, the new normal; surprisingly few manufacturers or integrators are well prepared for it.

The business models involved are fundamentally different as recurring revenue becomes king alongside customer retention, renewal rates and working capital. Monthly Recurring Revenue (MRR), Churn and Net Promotion Score (NPS) are becoming your new key KPIs.

In the traditional business models, manufacturing companies' processes are quite linear and self-centric. This means that the product development, sales, distribution, and order-to-cash processes drive the entire company's performance. The manufacturing company is also at the centre of its partners' and resellers' ecosystems.

By contrast, in an As-A-Service environment, the necessary processes are circular, and ecosystems are broader and less manufacturer-centric. Let me have a shot at listing the areas where the impact and the need for change are the highest now!

1. Product R&D
Solution Development is not limited to Product R&D but includes a comprehensive set of products, including software as well as services. It can be a challenge to deliver properly both at the start and at the end of the usage cycle, especially if the products are spread across multiple locations and markets.

2. Sales
The sales approach needs to be fundamentally reviewed, as the recognition and value system evolves. Sales teams won't be chasing one-off big deals generating large commissions; instead, companies need a more cohesive, company-wide approach aimed at satisfying and retaining the customer over a long period of time. This is the rise of our dearest Customer Success Managers.

3. Distribution
I have doubts about the role of the distribution channel. What is the role and profile of the channel partner going forward? How is it incentivized in the business origination and throughout the lifecycle of a subscription?

4. Order to cash
The order-to-cash process is quite different. The notion of an order itself is challenged as, in most cases, the subscription is not a firm commitment from the customer. In other words, I have to share the difficult news that the revenue varies according to the consumption and retention rate of the users.

5. Partnerships
The ecosystem in which the manufacturer operates is also broader and more collaborative in order to deliver a complete offer including integrated services of third parties. Companies need the ability to develop successful new organizational and other go-to-market strategies. On the legal side, they need the ability to weave end user, funder and service provider requirements into key documents.

6. Accounting
When it comes to accounting, they need to find new ways to optimize revenues and new balance sheet strategies. The accounting department and operational teams also need to track assets, manage asset lifecycle and monitor asset usage. Companies need to develop the ability to incorporate predictive behaviours into the pricing model used for performance. Here I open a wide door to data scientists and data management.

7. Full-service customer experience
In the past, factory-less product firms already acknowledged the fact that product development plays a far more critical role in the value chain than manufacturing operations, and Steve Jobs changed the world by focusing on the customer experience of the product. The next generation, while focusing on the customer experience, is already becoming sensitive to a full-service customer experience in-

volving greater challenges to integrate and scale up all the services included in the value chain.

8. Corporate Social Responsibility

One of the main benefits of the move to As-A-Service is that manufacturers or service providers have to manage the entire asset lifecycle. They retain ownership of their assets until the end of their life cycle and need to manage their disposal in a responsible and eco-friendly way. Currently, 60% of products reaching the end of their life are not recycled, composted or turned into reusable materials as stated in the report on Circular Economy "Eurostat waste statistics" of Ellen McArthur Foundation. I am so excited and energized by the fact that the move to As-A-Service models is an opportunity to rethink our economic future and finally make the "circular economy" a reality!

All these fundamental changes that I have tried to summarise will affect the way product companies are organized and radically transform their capability and financial profile.

This all means that companies need to develop a full set of new capabilities in order to remain relevant to their customers. They need to perform critical assessments to find solutions to the new challenges they face. Aligning market needs and value propositions to this essential market development is key.

Is As-A-Service leading to a societal revolution?

I am often performing the exercise of projecting myself and my customers into an As-A-Service based economy and society. The benefits of the move to As-A-Service to the users and hopefully to the environment are clear. A full service, with a flexible and convenient offering, coupled with a great, long-standing customer experience and responsible disposal of the assets at the end of their life are among the great bonuses that this evolution (or revolution) brings.

However, the investments required to develop utility-like, and multi-country As-A-Service solutions is complex; the market needs to consolidate and end up with fewer players. This accelerates the trend witnessed with the tech giants and their Chinese counterparts.

The battle for control of the end customer is engaged. It's unlikely that most customers care about the brand of car that the Uber driver is driving, the brand of power generator that the utility company is using, or the brand of server that the IT-cloud company is using.

So, will this As-A-Service based economy prevail? What will society look like in a full As-A-Service ground? What if there is no asset ownership to anchor society anymore? This may result in a more nomadic society, shorter economical life cycles and bigger swings from one successful provider to the next. Once again, the trend of As-A-Service will amplify the ability to adjust to an ever-changing world, the one in which we live as managers, consumers and human beings.

I appreciate the fact that this first book about the road to a successful, scalable and circular As-A-Service business model is available. Yann explores all of these conundrums and their possible consequences while providing some insights on how to initiate your As-A-Service journey. All this combined with personal experiences that make the reading of this book a pleasant experience. But be careful, As-A-Service is addictive and when you have finished this book, there will be no way back!

17

Can you leave it to someone else to manage the products you use? The world of business is in a stage of revolution, and only those companies who evolve will prevail.

Joseph Pulicano is a Managing Director in Accenture's Specialty Finance practice which helps Equipment Finance, Auto Finance and Product companies develop their future strategies and acquire or enhance new digital capabilities.

His experience spans across Managed Services, Equipment Finance and Consulting. He held senior leadership roles both in Europe and the USA. He successfully led all aspects of business transformation, including assisting several global firms to define and implement their As-A-Service strategy.

Introduction: Sailing without a boat

I'm on vacation in Brittany. I want to go sailing, but I don't have a boat. Where can I find a decent boat that I can use for just a day?

It's one of those glorious summer days; I am in St. Malo, going back to my roots with my partner. Growing up in this town by the sea, I developed a passion for sailing and I never miss an opportunity to go out when I'm near a coastline.

I just love St. Malo: strategically-placed on the Breton coast in France, its windswept medieval ramparts and ancient Roman walls are steeped in history – a history of intrepid endeavor, warfare and French corsairs. Perhaps this is what gave me my love of travel and a taste for exploring.

We're sitting at a café terrace opposite the harbor where hundreds of boats are moored, enjoying a refreshing drink and the cool sea breeze. Seeing the boats, I'm getting a bit restless: I need some action. I check the weather forecast on my phone. The conditions are ideal: sunshine, moderate breeze (4 on the Beaufort scale) and a tide that will allow me to leave the harbor at dawn. Perfect.

However, having lived in the Netherlands for the past 12 years, I'm no longer a local in St. Malo. As a visitor, it's virtually impossible to find a boat at the last minute. Still, I'm determined to go sailing, so my partner can experience that magical feeling of freedom out on those special seas.

Suddenly I remember an app that puts boat-owners in touch with sailing enthusiasts, based on the sharing economy model (www.clickandboat.com). I download the app, quickly set up my profile and look for boats available. My hopes aren't high. I mean, let's face it: who in their right mind is going to hand over their expensive boat to a total stranger? And, even though you don't need a license to sail a boat, you at least need some experience and to be able to handle potentially challenging weather conditions.

To my surprise, there are five boats available in St Malo that day. It still seems too good to be true, and I'm convinced that some savvy marketer has put those pictures of boats on my screen just to keep me on the app. Despite these misgivings, I decide to give it a shot and contact the owner of the best boat on offer. Within minutes of sending a message via the app, I receive an answer from Guillaume; his boat is available the next day. He even tells me where it's moored, so I can go and see it right away.

My heart starts to race; I feel like a kid on Christmas Eve. I pay the bill and almost run to the harbor. There she is, in all her glory. A two-year-old, 36-foot cruiser. I contact Guillaume to say we have a deal; he tells me where to find the keys and that I can take the boat right away if I want. After sorting out a few admin details on the app, I'm all set.

The next day, as I steer this fantastic boat out of the harbor – only a few hours after opening the app – I'm wondering how the hell all this is possible. How did Guillaume provide me with access to his boat so easily and seamlessly?

When I lived here as a kid, you needed your own boat to go sailing. **23** Here I am, in the same place, with the same boats, but the entire model has changed. And that's how, for the very first time, I person-ally experienced the shift from ownership to usership.

This book is about that very shift, which is completely changing in-dustry after industry.

I'd like to take you on a journey into this new world, using real-life examples and best practices of successful companies, who have al-ready taken this step into providing usership rather than transfer-ring ownership. Each concept in this book is presented as 'snack-able' content. Case studies are followed by a "behind the scenes explanation", as well as practical tips for implementing them in your business. Feel free to jump from one chapter to another or dip in and out as you please.

How can you turn your product-based business into a subscription model providing usership? I promise inspiration and practical tips you can use on your journey towards an As-A-Service business model. Be warned: you may discover a completely new way of looking at your business.

The central question shouldn't be *if* you should start this new approach but *when*. Next fiscal year? The next strategic plan? Or today? Because one thing's for sure: if you don't move ahead, your competitors will.

Show me the limits: What is As-A-Service?

It's not the As-A-Service model itself that is new, but the areas and industry sectors it's being applied to – ones that were unthinkable until recently.

We've been using the concept for decades, applying it in many forms to objects like company cars, copiers, printers and even coffee machines. Or simply by borrowing books via the public library. More recently in the software world, we've become familiar with subscription models such as Audible, which provides audiobooks, or Headspace for guided meditation.

From Blu-ray to Netflix

Back in 2010 while being in Paris, I had a conversation with a salesman in Fnac, a French book, DVD and CD chain. I was intrigued by Blu-ray technology, and wanted to find out more about it. He said that in his opinion, there was no point explaining the improved sound and vision quality because it required a substantial hardware investment to fully benefit from it. I was rather taken aback that he didn't even attempt to sell me a Blu-ray player!

He went on to explain – somewhat dejectedly but with what turned out to be surprising foresight – that Blu-ray was the last vestige of a dying technology trend, one in which films and TV series were stored on physical media and that the way forward was streaming. At the time of course, neither of us knew that Netflix was about to take the market by storm.

Netflix is a game-changer, in that they have shown the world that you can turn an entire industry into a subscription model in less than a decade. They have single-handedly ushered in the new As-A-Service era. The potential is obvious – and yet, only a fraction of this potential has been tapped into in terms of the types of industry to which the model can be applied. The opportunities are, therefore, huge.

Origins

The concept of As-A-Service originated in the IT industry. With the advent of cloud computing and remote access - offered as a subscription - IT vendors have changed their business models, switching from licensing software to subscription-based. By doing so, they have shown how a transactional business model can be turned into a subscription model.

As-A-Service went on to become a buzzword that was bandied about at every board meeting: it's become the holy grail of new business models. However, the concept itself remains somewhat nebulous. Board members of companies want to make it happen, because it generates recurring revenue, helps retain clients and increases shareholder value. Customers, meanwhile, want it because they prefer to just use a product or solution without the hassle and expense that comes with ownership. In both cases, the term is used to cover a multitude of ideas, ranging from a basic lease to a fully flexible subscription model.

Although it seems that everybody wants As-A-Service, between C-level and the customer there is a layer of management and their operational teams who have to put it in place. They have to tackle the challenge of defining what is or isn't included in the As-A-Service offering before they implement it – and they need to do this regardless of the legacy culture of the company and its associated points of resistance.

Four principles

To define As-A-Service more precisely and start working out how you can turn your product-based business into a subscription model, let's look at four examples at each end of the spectrum.

1. Pay-per-use or flat rate?
At one end of the spectrum is the electricity model that you use at home, which is a true pay-per-use model: you start paying when you

turn on the lights and stop when you switch them off. At the other end are offers whereby you pay a flat rate per month for "unlimited" use – but with certain restrictions. This is the case with Netflix, where you don't pay per movie or hour, but on a fixed monthly basis. For example, if I'm offline and don't watch any movies for three weeks, I still pay my subscription, whether I use it or not.

2. How many services are included?

Another way to look at the limits of an As-A-Service offer is to consider the amount – and type – of services included in the offer. Spotify, for example, gives you access to music and services as part of its package. You can follow artists and proactively share new releases and tour dates. Spotify introduces you to new music and artists by monitoring your musical tastes and preferences. It suggests playlists and allows you to share music with your friends.

Other examples include those with a broad service offering, such as car leasing. The types of services included vary from admin to hands-on support. Car lessors offer a wide range of services including insurance, registration, fuel card, monitoring, winter tires and roadside assistance, as well as a host of services to keep you mobile.

Another possible service to include in the As-A-Service offer is an enriched experience, based on data generated by end-users (in the same way that Audible recommends books based on your previous purchases).

The types of services that are suggested for inclusion in the As-A-Service offer will depend on the creativity of the teams that are in charge of developing these offers. In the USA, I have seen a hairdresser offer combined with a car-leasing offer. The driver of the car is invited once a month to the dealer to have his car cleaned and at the same time, to get a haircut!

3. Does it include a device?

An important question to bear in mind is whether or not there's a device included. Some As-A-Service solutions work with your own device, while others, such as Sonos Flex or Swapfiets (a Dutch company offering a bike-rental subscription service), provide you with a device with which to use the service. In the case of Swapfiets, the device (a bike) is the most important component of the service. The offer also includes repairs, insurance and replacement. Whatever the solution, if there's a tangible asset, such as a device or piece of equipment, it remains the property of the solution provider – which has considerable implications regarding the risks associated with retaining the ownership that are described later in this book. When a Spotify user stops paying, Spotify stops their service and that's it. However, it's a different story with a car-leasing company or Swapfiets; when their user stops paying, they have to take various measures – invariably involving logistics and costs – to collect their product.

4. As-A-Service for free?
A last point to consider is whether users can use a platform or a product free of charge. This is the case with Facebook or LinkedIn, for example. Just by having users on the platform generating content and providing data, the provider benefits. Such platforms make their profits by monetizing the community and the data collected. This is the ultimate As-A-Service offer on the market: use the service free by generating valuable data.

31

Once you apply these four principles to a product-based business model, the blue oceans in your industry soon become apparent. Do you make washing machines? Offer Washing-As-A-Service. Do you sell shaving products? Do Shaving-As-A-Service. The possibilities are endless.

I remember having dinner with the board of the Amsterdam Arena to celebrate a deal we had closed for IT Storage As-A-Service with my team at Econocom. Emboldened by a few glasses of wine, I asked what they'd like to see as the next As-A-Service model. After a few seconds of silence and exchanging some mischievous looks with his team, Henk Markerink, the CEO of the Arena, said to me:, "Yann, we'd love to hear about Lawn-As-A-Service for our stadium!" So, if any gardening firms are reading this book, give me a call and we'll start 'Lawn-As-A-Service'!

Bringing the kids to school

Every morning when I see my kids off to school, the sight of them loading their huge satchels bulging with books onto their bicycles never fails to dismay me. Ten to fifteen kilos of static, analog content to haul back and forth every day; there has to be another way! Has nothing changed in the 30 years since I was at school? There's something seriously wrong here...

My kids and their friends spend all their time on their smartphones and tablets watching YouTube while they do their homework, effortlessly juggling two or three devices at a time. They also receive hundreds of WhatsApp messages every hour. They are digital natives and their brains are hard-wired to handle the huge volumes of content delivered to them. Yet unbelievably, when it's time to go to school, it's as though they have stepped back in time to some pre-digital era. Basically, from 8am to 4pm, my kids are in a digital dead zone – despite the potential benefits of using new technologies when it comes to learning languages, math, history and geography.

Stranger in a Strange Land

Having lived abroad for several decades, I'm used to observing life from the sidelines. It gives me the opportunity to observe habits that are deeply rooted in a culture or a society from an outsider's perspective. When I see things that strike me as nonsensical and, more importantly, when these things are widely accepted and embraced, I just have to do something about it.

Together with my teams at Econocom, we made such observations and concluded that there was a gap in the education market that needed to be addressed. Students were asking for digital learning methods, teachers were open to implementing them, and the school governors wanted to bring these new solutions into the classroom.

So why isn't it happening? Why haven't classrooms and learning methods gone digital? Why must my kids undergo this enforced digital deprivation for eight hours a day? Why don't they get the chance to learn in a format that is in tune with their everyday life outside school, today's society and their future professional life?

The conclusion of our research and observations was that people are still weighing up the pros and cons of e-learning. I won't get into the debate here: suffice to say, we noticed that whenever a school decides to switch to e-learning, they soon find themselves embroiled in a project that's too vast and complex to implement and manage. This is because e-learning involves coordinating a whole lot of components: quite apart from changing the teaching program and mindset, you also need e-learning software, tablets, digital whiteboards, a decent Wi-Fi connection, continuity of service, training, and so on. It takes a massive investment in terms of both money and effort, for a school to kick off such a project and to keep the solution up and running. And once it's launched, they also have to think about regular software and technology upgrades.

Switching to e-learning is a major step for a school and this journey should not be underestimated. When the solution doesn't deliver on its promises – despite the best intentions and efforts of all the teaching and technical teams involved – the project will fail. Most schools don't have the resources to manage such a project. What we often see is that the person in charge of IT and digitization at a school is the math teacher, who has to try to crowbar these technical considerations into an already jam-packed agenda.

35

My team and I quickly spotted an opportunity to deliver value to schools by combining all the components needed to deliver e-learning and offering them in a subscription model. Based on these observations, we decided to organize all the components of an e-learning solution for schools and present them on a silver plate, neatly packaged as 'Classroom-As-A-Service'.

What happens in the e-school kitchen?

A school needs to be able to rely on the solution so they can focus on educating their students. How can you organize the backstage aspects to ensure a seamless on-stage experience?

The starting point is the content and the software that delivers the e-learning experience. After looking at various players on the market we decided to join forces with Gynzy (www.gynzy.com). They shared our vision of delivering a complete solution to schools.

Once we'd agreed on the content, we went to work on the hardware components. We contacted major manufacturers like Apple and Samsung to get them on board for delivering the tablets.

The next challenge involved checking the performance of Classroom As-A-Service, because it's all about service continuity. We needed to be absolutely sure that the solution would still perform when tablets were broken or (worse still) stolen, the Wi-Fi connection was poor, the software wasn't updated in time and all the other possible scenarios that could affect the solution's performance. We decided to bear these risks as a company and to combine it with excellent back-to-back contracts with all the different suppliers involved.

However, before we could start building Classroom As-A-Service, we had to tackle the issue of solvency risk. What if the school stops paying their fee because of cash-flow issues, when we've already made all the upfront software, tablet and service investments? As it turned out, it was relatively easy to address solvency risk, since schools' credit rating is pretty stable and easy to access. We decided to work with a financial partner to underwrite the risk and agreed on an approach to covering the risk for any school – unless they were blacklisted by the Ministry of Education.

By taking all the responsibility for the software, technology, performance of the solution and solvency risk, we made sure that schools could focus on their core activity, educating kids.

When it came to pricing the model, we found a clever solution that is our own in-house recipe that won't be fully disclosed in this book. We offer the complete solution for only €8 per student per month, including a 90-day trial period. Being the first player to bring a complete e-learning solution as a subscription to the education market is quite something!

To meet demand, we've teamed up with the sales team of our software supplier Gynzy and developed a portal through which schools can easily register for the solution online. Within two weeks of approving the solution, it's being delivered and implemented at the school.

I believe that Econocom's added value is that we have been the enabler that connects all the dots of the solution and also takes the risks that no other player is willing to take: performance and solvency. Econocom isn't a manufacturer, bank or software developer. Econocom is the business partner that combines all the necessary expertise and turns it into a monthly subscription model – while bearing all the associated risk and focusing on the end-user experience.

Unfortunately, my kids are already too old to be able to benefit from this solution, but about 30,000 younger kids enjoy it every day in the Dutch market.

Many bricks in the wall: Services around your product

You already have a product. How can you turn it into a service? An As-A-Service offer defines itself by the number of service components included in that offer. Since this book is mainly for product-based businesses, the first component to build the offer around is of course, the product. The chapter "What hardware to include" is dedicated to choosing the right product to include in your offer; for now let's focus on the services.

The next logical question is what to offer along with the product. When you're used to a transactional business model, i.e. selling a product and transferring ownership, it's not always easy to come up with a product/service combination for a complete user experience.

Well, I've got good news: you can call off the search. You're already delivering services with your products.

There are three service components that are most commonly offered in a traditional sale, which can be used as the first building blocks of your As-A-Service offer:

1. The advice you traditionally give when choosing from your different solutions
2. The installation/deployment of the solution
3. The maintenance/services provided to maintain the solution in good operational conditions

To ignite your As-A-Service offer you could include two more components:

4. Usage monitoring
5. Product refresh in 3-5 years

By bundling these five components plus your product and offering them in a monthly subscription, you already have an As-A-Service solution.

This basic format is your starter As-A-Service solution. It's a simple way to move from a transactional business model to an As-A-Service one, by retaining ownership and offering usership. Of course, some issues have to be addressed, such as the potential financial impact, new risks for your business and new revenue recognition models – but we'll come back to that later.

Any component of your As-A-Service solution is worth looking into to deliver maximum value to your customers – sorry, I mean your *users*!

You can do things differently to what you are already doing, with an As-A-Service angle. For example, let's take a closer look at the advice part. The first service major manufacturers offer is help in choosing the solution and integrating it in the customer's existing environment. This advice/design approach could also include collecting the customer's old products and handling recycling. This makes even more sense if it's an existing customer who already uses your products. You will get rid of their old equipment, as with a solution-based offer, the equipment will remain the property of the manufacturer or supplier of that solution. You've already taken a load off their mind by offering to handle the hassle of disposal for them.

Taking it one step further, you can get your existing customers to opt for an As-A-Service offer by applying the model to existing products, which can either be your own or your competitors'. In this case, you can buy the customer's products from them and then offer them back the usage of those products as part of an As-A-Service package. The products themselves, of course, will physically stay where they are – with the customer. The only thing that changes is the way they're serviced and who owns them.

This is one of the easiest ways to start your As-A-Service go-to-market. It's a bold move: claim back ownership of the goods you or your competitor have supplied to your customers for the last three years and instantly provide usership via an As-A-Service model. You will get rid of the competitors' presence faster, provide cash injections to your client, and plan refresh and deployments of your solution for the coming year. That's how you get into usership by the front door!

Service with a pen or a screwdriver

Another angle from which to approach an As-A-Service offer is to slice the user experience in four areas of services: technical, administrative, content and data-related.

1. Technical

I often say to my teams that we deliver two types of services: the ones that need a pen and the ones that need a screwdriver. The services that need a screwdriver are basically any sort of technical intervention on your product i.e. installation, maintenance, repairs, upgrades and collection when it's time to refresh the assets. All of these require the services of a technical expert.

They're crucial landmarks along the customer journey since they are touch-points with your customers. As such, they are opportunities to under-promise and over-deliver, gauge customer satisfaction and keep them updated on your latest offers, thus generating potential up- and cross-selling opportunities.

Note that it's also key to train your technical staff to interact in a different way with your customers. What do you do if the equipment needs major maintenance or repairs and the refresh time frame you've promised is in three months' time? Will you go ahead with the major maintenance operation or upgrade to a new product? Your technical staff has to address customer issues in a completely new way.

2. Administrative

Services requiring a pen are the administrative ones included in your offer, for example insurance for your products, fleet management and reports, specific invoicing to different business units, or managing the offer in different countries for your international customers.

Product insurance is a must-have for your As-A-Service offer: you need to be able to replace any damaged, broken or stolen products. I remember delivering digital tablets for an As-A-Service solution once; ten of them were stolen during a seminar the customer held (the meeting room door was left open during the lunch-break). Why should the customer go on paying for the solution when the main asset – the tablets – is no longer available? You can get sucked into endless discussions with your customers if you don't provide a solution to cover any damage or theft of the equipment and thus ensure uninterrupted service delivery.

3. Content-related

Content-based services depend on the type of product you're offering, and what that product is used for. In the case of Classroom-As-A-Service for example, the tablets we delivered with Econocom are mainly used for e-learning. The content is, therefore, the main driver for this offer; the schools aren't looking for tablets but for e-learning. Think about what your customers will use your products for. If it's to play music - join forces with a streaming company. If they want to do 3D printing, team up with the provider of the "ink" and the software to do this. The more value you provide in the chain of service and content around your product, the more customers will buy into this seamless experience.

On a recent trip to Asia, I used a taxi service called Grab. Unlike Uber - which I regularly use because it's easy and available almost anywhere in the world - Grab doesn't include a payment option: you have to pay the driver in cash at the end of the fare. This means a poorer user experience, especially when you're in a hurry and dealing with an unfamiliar currency. This is a concrete example of how just one service can make an offer stand out: Uber went one step further by including payment.

4. Data-related

Services including a digital component create interaction between the user and the company, based on the data generated by the user. For example, if you provide your solution via an online platform or app, or if your product collects use-based data, you'll gather key data for your business. These data will give you valuable insights into how your solution is being used, which will in turn enable you to enhance the customer experience. Take the example of Spotify recommending tracks you might like, based on your playlist: the data you collect will also give you a better idea of what services to deliver.

If you offer Washing Machines-As-A-Service, the data you collect should tell you what type of program your user uses the most, so you can even advise them on another program that will save water, as well as delivering washing powder before they need to order some more.

You'll also be able to advise the user on the best solution when they upgrade, since you'll have gleaned plenty of insights into the way they use it.

The services you choose to deliver will be organized either in-house or via partnerships with other suppliers. The choice of in-house or outsourced services will affect various aspects of the solution – including your ability to cover performance risk, which will be covered in a later chapter.

44   Choosing which services should be the foundation when launching your As-A-Service offer isn't rocket science; just focus on the services you already deliver in a traditional way and incorporate the same ones but based on use of the products. That way, you'll already have a solid base from which to start offering solutions instead of products. Get one of your best customers on board by offering to turn the products they're already using into a usership offer, and you've got your first win!

I want to ride my bicycle

Amsterdam is renowned for its large number of bicycle commuters. The bicycle is the main means of transportation for Dutch people. Whatever the weather, Dutch people go to work by bike, take their kids to school by bike, do their grocery shopping by bike and they even go out to dinner by bike.

Dutch people take bicycles very seriously. It's not a toy or a hobby, but one of their key transportation solutions. The whole country is organized to ensure easy, safe biking: cycle lanes are everywhere and completely separate from the rest of the car or pedestrian traffic. I can still remember how surprised I was the first time I saw a snow plough clearing a cycle lane one snowy morning.

Needless to say, every Dutch citizen owns at least one bike, thus the average spend per capita on acquiring and maintaining bicycles is considerably higher than in other countries.

For years, the bicycle market was driven by ownership and the Dutch were very attached to owning their bicycle; the market didn't seem open to a usership model.

In the past few decades, a number of big cities worldwide have started offering bike-sharing solutions. Mobike, for example, provides a dockless bike-sharing platform in a number of cities (mobike.com/global). For a fee (charged per minute of use) you just find a Mobike near you, unlock it, and you're good to go. However, until recently, this type of solution hadn't made it onto the Dutch market as the Dutch preferred to use their own bike.

One of the pictures tourists like to take in Amsterdam is the bike parking area at the Central Station; thousands of bikes are parked there and foreign visitors are always amazed to see so many in one place. It has even been said that there are more bikes in the country than people! One of the questions tourists always ask is, "How do you find your bike in this jungle of bikes?"

About two years ago, as I was passing the bike park, I noticed that one of the bicycles had a bright blue front tire. I thought how clever the owner was to put a different color on the front tire so it would stand out. A few days later, I noticed more bicycles around town with blue front tires. Something was up. I asked around to find out if other people had also noticed the tires and a friend mentioned that those bikes were offered in an As-A-Service model. It is called Swapfiets, (swapfiets.nl – *fiets* means bicycle in Dutch). Personally, I didn't think its chances for success were very high; how would Dutch people shift from ownership to usership?

However, these days, when you walk around Amsterdam you'll see bikes with blue front tires everywhere. The offer has found its market, and more and more people are now using their bicycle instead of owning it.

Swapfiets offers two models of bikes, with prices varying from one city to another. In Amsterdam, prices range from €16.90 to €59.90 a month, depending on the bike you choose. The minimum contract duration is one month, with a one-month notice period. Everything is managed via an app so the user can connect directly with Swapfiets for any questions or issues.

49

The Swapfiets offer or their 'promise', is this: as soon as you sign up to the service via their app, you get your own Swapfiets bicycle delivered free: just say where and when. The subscription includes a lifetime warranty. If you have an active subscription, Swapfiets handles all your bicycle repairs. If your Swapfiets bike is broken, they'll deliver a replacement to your home within a day. Even if the bike is stolen, you will be provided a new one for a small fee - depending on your subscription.

In terms of the mechanics of the offer, Swapfiets retains ownership of the equipment i.e. the bike and offers the user a complete service to ensure hassle-free, continuous use. This involves bearing the various risks – solvency, performance, etc. – in order to provide the cyclist with a seamless experience. The fact that Swapfiets also offers complete interaction via an app makes communication between the user and the supplier child's play.

I like the example of Swapfiets because it shows how an apparently closed, ownership-driven market can be converted to a usership market. The entrepreneurs behind the concept are three students from the University of Delft: Richard Burger, Martijn Obers and Dirk de Bruijn. They initially targeted students, but the ease of the solution has meant that many expats signed up and now it seems like everyone is using it.

Another reason I like the Swapfiets case is that they've created a new way of using bicycles in a market that, from the outside, did not look ready for such an offer. This is an inspiration and a great example to follow when it comes to finding a blue ocean in your industry; what do people or organizations use on a daily basis that could be offered as a subscription, all services included, to provide a comprehensive experience?

It's also interesting to note that Swapfiets is the brainchild of three young entrepreneurs and not a bike manufacturer. As with many As-A-Service offers, the manufacturers aren't offering their own products via these models; instead, intermediaries are taking the lead. This means that either you take your hard-earned market presence and turn it into an As-A-Service model, or you can wait for an external player to step in and disrupt your market, sooner and faster than you may imagine.

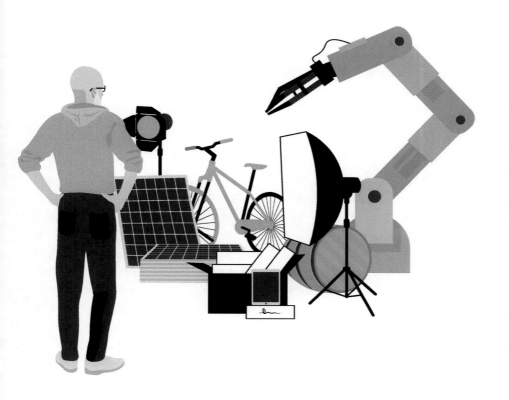

What hardware to include?

I arrived at the office one morning, grabbed a delicious coffee (from the As-A-Service coffee machine that was part of the "hospitality at work" program), walked through the open space and ran straight into Robert, our CTO. He was looking rather ashen-faced and the news he gave me made me conclude that my perfect day was over almost before it had even started. Apple had apparently just announced they were discontinuing the iPad mini – practically overnight.

This had huge implications for Econocom; our Classroom-As-A-Service offer was based on the iPad mini. Everything we had put together – financially, technically and in terms of service – was falling apart in one fell swoop.

We eventually solved this by offering the customers the choice between a new bigger iPad and a Samsung tablet. Conclusion: using two brands prevents dependence on the technical roadmap of the manufacturers.

That's when I realized something about the type of hardware, the choice of manufacturer, and dependency on a single type of product – all these are risks that need to be mitigated. The hardware, the product that is part of your As-A-Service offer, has to fulfil certain criteria in order to mitigate risks, offer a great user experience and generate other types of income streams than the ones you usually get from your services.

If you're a manufacturer, obviously your own products will do the job; the following tips therefore apply to the software and service providers you'll select to make your As-A-Service offer complete.

Choose well-known

First, I strongly advise going for the best-known brands and the most common types of products. When you choose "exotic" assets or brands that don't have a proven track record, you expose yourself to performance issues, technical road map surprises and potentially bad surprises on the second life cycle or the second-hand market valuation at the end of the service cycle.

For example, if your model includes tablets, go for the main manufacturers – Apple, Samsung or Microsoft. Even with known brands you can have surprises, as we did with the discontinuation of the iPad mini, which wasn't announced in advance. This is very unusual and is not expected to happen again. However, you can mitigate the risk by using multiple suppliers for the same type of device. You already have enough on your plate delivering the promise to your customers without having to worry about performance and reliability issues.

Don't put yourself in a situation where you could be faced with poor performance, a manufacturer roadmap that's not clearly defined - resulting in continuity issues in your offer - or hardware-related maintenance problems. Remember you'll soon have a large fleet of devices to manage. So go for standardization and clear roadmaps where product upgrades are concerned, and lasting relationships with hardware suppliers. In short, you need to team up with the best-in-class in your industry.

Core business

When selecting which hardware or product to include in your As-A-Service offer, it also needs to be central to your customer's core business. An organization that relies on your product and services to run its business will keep paying your rentals, no matter what.

Let's take the example of customers who use devices to collect payment, such as check-out systems in supermarkets. Obviously, the closer the service you offer is to your customer's core business, the more likely they are to pay you. You need to ask yourself, "What if this customer can't use my service or devices anymore? Will they stop being able to collect payment from their end-clients? Will they have difficulty delivering their services?"

Projects such as printing systems for newspapers are at the core of their business; if they don't have the printers anymore, they are out of business. I have been involved in another interesting project run by a software provider that offers multimedia experiences for hospital patients. They started with content only. Then they offered to include the hardware to display this content. In other words, they offered the hospitals a complete solution by including bedside terminals and TVs in the offer. The hospital then charges their patients a fee for the usage of this solution.

These are all examples where it is guaranteed the customer will keep paying you rentals because the assets provided are key to their business.

Connectivity

Having central control over the use of the products will give your As-A-Service far greater value.

Firstly, you'll be able to collect information on the use of your solutions, which will enable you to increase the customer experience by being constantly in tune with their needs.

Imagine, for example, you're offering Solar Panels As-A-Service. Knowing how much electricity the equipment produces and the proportion of it that is being re-injected to the grid will enable you to proactively serve your customers better. You could offer to provide tips to get the most out of the solution, and advice on the best equipment to choose when it's time to refresh.

Back on the example of Washing Machines-As-A-Service. In a way, you're building a community of washing machine users based on the data you'll collect. This community and the way you address it is your next challenge and opportunity. See what a world of difference there is between just selling a washing machine and maybe throwing in a maintenance contract, to monitoring the end user's washing experience and guaranteeing them clean laundry at all times for the best price, conditions, and service level.

Secondly, in the event that your customer stops paying your rentals for whatever reason, it's an enormous advantage to be able to remotely control the assets that are spread over a wide geographical area, enabling you to take action quickly. By remotely shutting down the use of your assets, you'll be able to recoup payment.

Of course, this would be impossible for some of the examples I cited earlier. You can't remotely shut down fitness equipment or, in the case of Swapfiets, bikes. A bedside entertainment terminal in a hospital on the other hand, can easily be switched off from a central point. If a customer of Energy As-A-Service is going out of business and stops paying, the supplier can remotely turn off the meters and the delivery of energy will be instantly turned off.

Connectivity is therefore key for increasing the customer experience and generating new business models such as monetizing your community of users and, of course, securing continuity of payment.

Collect and resell

It goes without saying that the hardware you provide needs to be mobile and not attached to a building or part of another asset that you don't own (a tracker on a truck, for example). That way you can retrieve the asset, either at the end of the contract or in the event of payment default.

Your ability to collect the asset and re-use it for a new cycle or sell it on the second-hand market will secure profit streams at the end of the life cycle. It will also mean you can monetize the assets in the event of payment default and thus reduce your potential losses.

Both performance risk and solvency risk can be mitigated if you're smart about which assets you choose when putting your solution together. This will ensure a better user experience and seamless management of large fleets of assets, thereby monetizing your community and providing strong collateral in the event of payment default.

Don't own
your car

Whenever I set foot in a country I don't know, one of the first ways I take the pulse of the country's economy is by checking out its car fleet. Some might call this short-sighted, but it provides valuable insights.

I usually arrive by plane so the first experience is the taxi ride from the airport and the cars I see on the road. I look at the level of maintenance of the vehicles, how clean they are, how old, whether minor everyday damages have been repaired, and so on. This way, I can get a pretty accurate idea of the state of the fleet and how it's serviced. These factors vary enormously from one country to another. As an added bonus, you get a cultural impression by seeing how local drivers behave in traffic.

When I'm in the Netherlands, I'm always impressed by the vehicles on the road. Schiphol, Amsterdam's airport, is well known for the Tesla taxis that always strike first-time visitors. So why is it that some countries have newer and more expensive car fleets than others? Aside from being related to the Gini index, (the "statistical dispersion intended to represent income inequality or wealth inequality within a nation or any other group of people" according to Wikipedia) another, more prosaic answer to this question is the market penetration level of car leasing companies.

When explaining the As-A-Service business model, people often compare it to car leasing, because it's something of a trail-blazer. I'm referring here to long-term (i.e. three-to-five years) car rental companies like ALD or LeasePlan, as opposed to short-term rental companies like Hertz or Sixt which handle short-term vehicle rentals (a few days to one month). It's crucial to understand how this market is organized in order to hold it up as an example for emerging As-A-Service markets.

Why lease and not own?

Firstly, let's look at the advantages of car leasing. Are you the driver of a leased car? Are you an entrepreneur managing a large fleet of vehicles? Using a leased car offers an essential service: mobility without the hassles associated with owning a car for the driver, and the freedom to focus on their core business for the entrepreneurs.

To enjoy these advantages and understand the business model, it's interesting to look at the range of services offered by car leasing companies. These can be divided into two main categories, as previously mentioned: pen or screwdriver. In other words, administrative services or technical services.

When it comes to "pen" services, car-leasing companies will advise you on which model and brand to choose, the tax system applied to these models and which options to choose. Once you've made your choice they'll handle procurement, registration, insurance and tax. Throughout the contract term, you'll be provided with additional services such as an analysis of your car park, driver behavior, fine management and claims management, as well as a petrol card and, above all, hassle-free access to all technical service providers.

This is where the screwdriver kicks in, for example, with easy swapping of your summer tyres for winter ones, broken windows repaired in a day, maintenance sorted with a simple phone call – even the use of a replacement vehicle in the event of minor repairs being required.

In other words, all these services are geared towards offering you a unique driving experience without the hassle. The cherry on the cake is that you can replace your vehicle with a new model every three to five years within the same budget – a perk that many companies include in their employee benefits package.

Partnerships

In the context of car leasing, the capital required to ensure investment in vehicles as well as the capacity to offer business continuity services cannot be provided by the car leasing companies alone. Therefore, they have to work with a number of partners.

As a great deal of capital is required, car rental companies are often subsidiaries of banks; ALD, for example, belongs to Société Générale. One of the only ways to secure financing for large car fleets – and therefore direct access to the capital – is through direct contact with major banking groups. This model therefore implies considerable dependence on banks.

On the other hand, one advantage of the long-term car-leasing model is that the main companies are all independent of car manufacturers, which means that the user can switch brands easily. First and foremost, car-leasing companies are service and product integrators who combine all the service providers under a single offer to provide the end user with a holistic mobility experience.

The economic model is thus driven mainly by the partnerships with the various partners and the resulting business volumes. As owners of massive fleets of vehicles, car rental companies are able to negotiate significant back margin terms (or affiliate commission) with their partners. For example, glass repair providers secure a volume of business by signing agreements with car leasing companies and transfer part of their profits in return. The main source of income for car leasing providers is back margin programs.

It is important to quickly reach a large installed base in order to generate economies of scale and have substantial negotiating power over the entire business ecosystem involved in your offer.

The partnership between the major car leasing companies and service providers such as Uber is a good example of how to do that. Uber wants to be able to offer passengers and drivers good-quality, latest-generation vehicles without owning them. Car rental companies, meanwhile, are looking to contract the biggest fleets possible to accentuate the effects of scale. Uber and the car rental companies have therefore formed a natural partnership whereby Uber can rent cars and offer them to its drivers. Uber deducts the leasing amount from each driver's turnover, and the deduction is made at source through Uber. If a driver doesn't make enough fares to pay for their car, Uber simply takes the car away and gives it to another driver. The solvency risk is thus covered for both Uber and the car leasing company. The car leasing company ends up with a large number of private individuals as end customers – but with the financial guarantee supplied by Uber. As for Uber, it can offer its new drivers a quality car, make it easier for new drivers to come on board and offer its customers a better-quality experience. For the car leasing companies, this is a shortcut to winning the race for the installed base, and benefiting from economies of scale.

Your 'homework'

The question that regularly arises when identifying a new market for an As-A-Service venture is, "Why have certain products or services become essential As-A-Service candidates while others are completely overlooked?" The next time you lease a car, I suggest you take a few minutes to list all the services included in the car leasing offer and then ask yourself why car leasing is the mobility solution you choose for your company instead of owning the cars.

I also invite you to think about your market position and the opportunities for becoming a service and product integrator, and thus a key As-A-Service player in your industry. Car leasing companies are neither car manufacturers nor service providers; their market is vast because they aren't dependent on a particular brand or technology.

Concerning your own model, aim wide: don't limit yourself to just your offer or product. Like car-leasing companies, the market may be much bigger than you initially think if you establish yourself as a leading As-A-Service provider in your industry, without being tied to a particular brand or service. Shoot for the moon: even if you miss, you'll land in the stars!

In-house or with partners?

Who will dare to make the first steps to offer the end user a complete As-A-Service experience?

As C-level or as an entrepreneur, we are often torn between day-to-day operations on the one hand and mid-term vision planning on the other. I often ask myself if I'm working *in* my business or *on* my business that day. Taking a step back from the day-to-day stuff is a great way to reflect and find ways to connect the dots – preferably in new ways. I force myself to set aside three days every quarter to brainstorm on my business, preferably in a different environment or even a foreign country. The headspace you create by literally taking a step back is a great way to boost creativity and discover dots that are ready to be joined.

When it comes to designing your As-A-Service offers, I strongly advise you to do the same. Take a few days off, bring a pencil and a sketchpad and map all the products and services that your end users need to make their experience of your product or service complete. That will give you a good idea of the players you need to team up with to offer a comprehensive As-A-Service solution. In other words, which services and products do you need to include in your As-A-Service offer to stand out in your ecosystem and become the single point of contact for both the users and the suppliers?

Turn it around

Let's go back to a previous example and imagine you are a washing machine manufacturer offering laundry As-A-Service: a Washing Machine-As-A-Service offer will include laundry supplies, of course! This means you'll quickly become a significant buyer in the laundry supplies market, which will give you negotiating power with the laundry detergent producers.

However, what if the laundry supplier decides to provide Laundry-As-A-Service and include washing machines in their offer? The angles used to offer As-A-Service solutions are often surprising. Ask yourself from which angle the As-A-Service offers you know have come: this could have been from the manufacturer, service provider, software provider, bank, supply provider, and so on and so forth.

Looking at many examples of successful As-A-Service offers, the player that stands out in the ecosystem is rarely the manufacturer of goods. Instead, it is often a service provider or independent player.

In any case, the business that dominates the ecosystem will become the essential service provider. By reaching this stage yourself, you'll be at the top of the value chain delivered to the end user and gain a certain control over the players in the ecosystem; you'll be at the top of the food chain! Just as I ask myself if I'm working *in* or *on* my business, you can ask yourself if you are *in* the ecosystem or *on* top of the ecosystem of your industry.

If you're a product manufacturer or service provider, you will probably have to offer your customers services that are somewhat remote from your core business. With Classroom-As-A-Service, for example, building the offer started with the maker of the e-learning software – which is a far cry from managing a Wi-Fi network or providing tablets and insurance to ensure a complete experience for the end user.

The issue of whether to use in-house expertise or join forces with different players in the ecosystem is in fact a no-brainer; the range of expertise needed to provide a satisfying experience for your end customer is very broad so it requires partnering with specialists. For example, would you be able to provide an insurance solution in case the products in your offer are stolen or damaged?

Your main objective is to quickly set up an installed base of significant size in order to benefit from economies of scale by providing large business volumes to the different parties you involve in your offer. Time is of the essence. The fastest way to do this is to work with partners, so you can provide services that you don't have in-house. This puts you at the top of the ecosystem. You can only do this once you have certain expertise in this industry.

67

At the top of the ecosystem you manage many players, both in house and with partners. If one of the partners doesn't deliver, everything collapses. This brings us to the performance risk challenges of being dependent on external service providers. Poor performance of just one of the players in your offer will invariably lead to customer satisfaction issues that could result in damage to your reputation, poor reviews and even customers withholding payment.

Choosing the right partners is thus key (see the chapter on performance risk). You will also need to understand your industry's best practices, so you can step in if one of your partners or suppliers doesn't deliver on its promise to the end user.

Having said that, managing a large portfolio of service providers and being seen as a thought leader also presents some interesting opportunities.

If you establish yourself as the go-to payment management solution provider for other service providers, they will be eager to work with you. As you become the main provider and buy products and services from the various players in the ecosystem, you'll establish yourself directly as a player that pays all its suppliers on time and in full, then takes care of collecting the funds on a month-to-month basis from your end customers. The service providers will therefore be grateful to you for taking care of end-customer solvency issues and avoiding late payment and collection problems.

Offering to be the go-to payment provider also gives you negotiating power, provided you quickly have a significant installed base. The solution provider and negotiating power go together; your partners will appreciate the work and risks you take away from them and will become dependent on you, which generally translates into margin retrocession programs based on volume.

Going back to the example of washing machines. If you buy five tons of laundry supplies a year, the purchase or margin retrocession conditions will naturally be in your favor. You will then have the choice of either benefitting from this margin in full or partially integrating it into your offer, thereby reducing the amount of the recurring fee you charge to your end customers and making your pricing very competitive.

This example illustrates the best practices you can implement to optimize your relationship with the various service providers in the ecosystem, and either benefit directly from this in your P&L or retrocede part of it to your end customers.

When taking the first steps and connecting the dots in order to offer the end user a complete As-A-Service experience, you'll need to join forces with other players in your ecosystem. Trying to do everything in-house will be a challenge since it will take a long time to service the installed base you need. Being *on* your ecosystem and managing all the different players will raise performance risk issues, but it will also provide opportunities to enhance your pricing and profitability since you will be able to focus on purchasing power. Either join forces with the leaders in your industry and thus secure the performance risk, or go for being the challenger, in which case you disrupt the business model and increase your margin.   **69**

Show me
the light

I'll never forget the day I heard that Schiphol, Amsterdam airport, had signed a contract with Philips for Light-As-A-Service. My first reaction was to think, "Of course, it's so obvious!" Schiphol is a real trailblazer in the field of digital airports and was bold enough to challenge Philips to provide light in a subscription model. This ground-breaking move revolutionized the lighting industry.

Philips likes to say that they have only one competitor: the sun. Perhaps this was the inspiration for the bold move towards Light-As-A-Service. Signify (formerly Philips Lighting) allows its customers to benefit from light without investing in the assets that deliver it. This model is called LaaS and it is literally booming!

Signify mainly targets B2B companies with substantial portfolios looking to switch to LED. Their offer is based on a strong business case. The initial advantage of Light-As-A-Service is that there's no need for an upfront capital investment to make the transition from traditional lighting to LED. Since the drop in energy consumption resulting from switching to LED is significant, the instant Return-on-Investment is a strong decision making factor.

Providing light for a monthly fee flattens costs and aligns them with the savings. The drop in energy consumption offsets the monthly cost, meaning customers can break even or even make a profit right from the first month of service. In other words, with Light-As-A-Service, the decision about whether or not to upgrade your lighting is something of a no-brainer.

This offer gets rid of the two main obstacles that often prevent companies from changing their lighting system: the basic investment amount and the fear that the technology will soon be replaced by something more energy-efficient.

This is how Signify sums it up on their website: "From the initial design and installation to operation and maintenance, we've got you covered. You get the service levels you deserve, and the system performance we've agreed to. With LaaS (Light-As-A-Service), you can generate instant savings and optimize your cash-flow from day one." (www.signify.com/global/lighting-services/managed-services/light-As-A-Service)

Based on this strong concept, Light-As-A-Service is becoming increasingly popular and competition has developed pretty fast. New players are popping up every day: a simple Google search on Light-As-A-Service currently comes up with 6,060,000,000 hits.

As competition increases, we are seeing a shift in the Light-As-A-Service market from a financing offer to a full service model. As the offer was initially designed mainly to optimize cash-flow, there were relatively few services offered. Now providers are becoming increasingly creative with their offers in an attempt to stand out. The offers range from a simple provision of equipment to the inclusion of services such as auditing, design, installation, maintenance, future upgrades and data services.

Some energy suppliers have even decided to offer their customers Light-As-A-Service, promising savings on their energy bill, as well as maintenance and possible improvements.

I'm always interested in investigating how a company or market has made the transition to an As-A-Service model. In the case of Light-As-A-Service, the initial driving force was a major technological breakthrough with the arrival of LEDs on the market. The benefits in terms of energy savings and asset life are obvious. Due to the desire to reduce energy consumption and meet their CSR targets, a number of light-intensive organizations have chosen to switch to LED. In order to accelerate the transition, lighting suppliers started to include financial offers to increase interest in switching without an initial investment. This in turn prompted the competition to develop packages that are more comprehensive, adding other services to the initial financial offer, making the on-demand lighting market what it is today. All this took about five years.

Circular economy

Signify has paved the way for Light-As-A-Service: this is one of the very few examples of a manufacturer taking the lead in providing its assets in a subscription model. In addition, since manufacturers are at the source of the offer, this creates great opportunities to enter into the circular economy model.

Light As-A-Service, for example, is perfectly in line with the principles of the circular economy. Firstly, the accelerated transition to new technologies helps to reduce energy consumption and electricity bills thereby achieving the objective of reducing greenhouse gas emissions. What's interesting is that Philips is motivated by a desire to produce more sustainable solutions and equipment that is easier to reuse, because it retains ownership. As Philips own the lights, once they're installed on the end-user's site it's in their best interests to ensure they last as long as possible and are not replaced.

Similarly, the principle of circularity was one of the main reasons for Schiphol's decision to sign a Light-As-A-Service contract: Philips commits to collecting any old lamps for reuse or recycling.

The example of Light-As-A-Service shows how a technological breakthrough (LED lighting) created a major financial advantage (a drop in energy consumption), which led to the development of As-A-Service offers to reduce the cash-flow impact. This in turn resulted in continually increasing levels of service as market players get more creative in their race for the largest installed base. This change resulted in a concentration of ownership of lighting assets among a handful of players. These players are now being forced to rethink the production of the equipment, as they retain ownership and are responsible for recycling old equipment.

This major shift in the way the light is being offered and used at Schiphol has been the inspiration for me and my team at Econocom to offer the same principle when it comes to the 5,000 displays at the airport: Display As-A-Service.

Technological obsolescence risk

We all remember Kodak and their dominant position in the photo industry – at least until the advance of digital cameras. A major technology breakthrough is always a turning point for a specific industry, and one that can provide an opportunity for, or have a devastating impact on certain players.

With As-A-Service, technological discontinuity is an essential challenge, as you remain the owner of thousands of products. If you choose to offer a flexible As-A-Service model – like Swapfiets, for example – with a one-month termination notice period, the obsolescence risk is fully yours. When a new technology comes on to the market, the one you offer to your users could become obsolete. In that case, you may find yourself with mass returns of your products, as users will want to terminate their contract and upgrade to the new technology. In addition, if one of your competitors offers this new product, you could lose customers and income and end up with a large fleet of obsolete assets on your hands that users haven't finished paying for.

78   A bleak scenario, you might say. But just imagine if Kodak had offered analog cameras as part of an As-A-Service package, with film and development included. What would have happened to all those cameras that users returned so they could enjoy the new digital ones? How could Kodak have recouped the sub-investments made upfront to be able to deliver the service? Maybe this would have forced them to offer digital cameras instead, in which case they would have still been in the same strong position.

And what if Sony had offered DVD Players-As-A-Service a few years before the launch of streaming solutions such as Netflix: would users have kept their DVD players for longer? If we take a closer look at Swapfiets, the same scenario could apply to their model. What if, in the next six months, electric bikes or motorized scooters become basic, affordable technology that cost the same as traditional bikes? What will Swapfiets do with its thousands of "analog" bikes?

So, how can you manage technological obsolescence risk with an As-A-Service solution including a product – hardware – that requires major upfront investments?

Technology watch

First and foremost, it's essential to dedicate some of your resources to investigating new technologies. This is already common practice in the ICT leasing industry: keeping an eye out for new technologies, how they're developing, how the market is reacting to them, and so on. It's not that different to competitor monitoring, which you certainly already do in your organization. Any new player in your market, any new technology and any new outsider should be on your radar and potentially lead to changes in your offer as soon as possible. Complacency or resistance to change are often key at this stage: don't be too comfortable in your position, as Kodak once were; don't be afraid to try new offers based on new products; run customer tests; and be ready for mass implementation.

Upgradeability and clear roadmap

The experience you deliver must be upgradable. You need to ensure the customer can enjoy your services in the long term: upgrade them on a regular basis, keep making improvements, and never stop developing new features and services along the way.

It can often be tempting for developers of solutions to provide customers and users with major upgrades. Users aren't always ready to take giant steps in the services they use; sometimes it's more customer-friendly to offer minor changes and upgrades. Where innovation is concerned, you've got to pace yourself: don't show all your cards at once. That way, you can avoid any major failures and make sure the customer stays interested, and you can keep up with your innovation curve, as is the case for software providers who distribute new features with a well-defined roadmap.

It is crucial to define a clear roadmap – on a three-year timeframe, for example – of how you're going to distribute the new features, options, and services that you'll eventually add. This roadmap should include the technical upgrades you plan to offer in the coming months and years. With a constantly up-to-date roadmap, you'll be able to stay one step ahead of any major technological changes. By delivering the subsequent features and options according to this roadmap, you'll be ready to step up the pace at any time in the event that a technological change arises in your industry sooner than expected.

Residual value: pace yourself

Offering a product As-A-Service means that you will collect the equipment at the end of the contract. You might offer it to another user, sell it on the second-hand market, incorporate it back into your production process or dismantle it for spare parts. The estimated future value of the asset can be deducted from the initial value and incorporated into your calculation of the monthly price you charge your users. For example, I have a tablet worth $300 and rent it out on a three-year contract. I know that the tablet will be worth $100 on the market when I get it back (this is called residual value.) I will then only charge my customer on a base of $200 for the three-year rental period.

It might be tempting to increase the residual value in order to boost your pricing model. Given the risk of obsolescence, calculation of residual value is essential. Because when you base your business model on the assumption that you'll make 10 to 30% income on the returned equipment at the end of the contract, you'd better make sure that they'll still be worth something by then.

If the technology changes in the meantime, the market value could be virtually non-existent – an additional headache - on top of the fact that your users will be returning the equipment early.

The trick is to strike the right balance so you don't end up with a residual value estimate that will be too high in the event of a major technological advance.

Time-to-market

Remember how slowly new technologies were adopted in the 80s? It took 30 years for televisions to come into households in Europe, ten years to upgrade from black-and-white to color, and five years to switch from traditional TVs to flat screens. The same could be said of a number of other technologies: GPS, Tablets, Wearables, Smartphones...

The implementation of new technologies – the time to market – is increasingly fast. Once a new technology hits the market these days, implementation takes only one to three years.

You always need to bear in mind that the technology you offer in an As-A-Service model could become obsolete within a year. So know your market and be ready to upgrade your offers and products according to a precise roadmap – without gambling too much on the market value at the end of the contract.

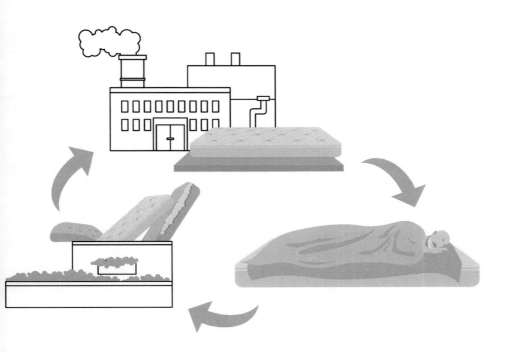

Sleep like a log

Quality of sleep is one of the main components of a happy, healthy life. I am surprised at how little attention we pay to the quality of our sleep. We may be aware that a good routine can ensure a good night's sleep but this requires a certain amount of discipline that is difficult to maintain. Avoiding heavy meals before bed, cutting down on coffee in the afternoon and turning off screens one hour before going to bed are all good practices I try to apply so that I wake up feeling great the next morning. However, we tend to overlook one important component in sleep that doesn't require a great deal of discipline: the quality of the bed you sleep in.

When you realize that we spend about a third of our life in bed, surely the bed should be the most important asset in your life. In Europe, the average lifespan of a bed is 13-14 years, whereas it ideally shouldn't exceed ten years. Compare that to a car, which is replaced every five years and in which we spend approximately two hours a day on average... And think now how much we spend on our car, compared to what we invest in our bed.

84 I've noticed that whenever I raise this subject with family and friends, replacing beds is something people tend to put off. It's mostly seen as a headache (too expensive, too much time and hassle).

This is where Auping saw an opportunity. They have been the Netherlands' leading bed manufacturer since 1888. By providing quality mattresses and box springs in a subscription model, Auping offers sleep As-A-Service to both companies and consumers. A good night's sleep thus becomes a service, like watching a film on Netflix. It's the same principle: you don't need a DVD, you just need to see a movie; and you don't need to own a bed, you just need a good night's sleep.

Sustainability

In addition to producing high-quality beds, Auping is renowned for its commitment to sustainability and the environment; the company is a "Certified Benefit Corporation" or B Corp, meaning it strives to maintain the highest standards of social and ecological perfor-mance, accountability and transparency.

In addition to offering a good night's sleep by providing quality bed-ding, they also ensure recycling. When the mattress reaches the end of its useful life, the service contract includes replacement and re-verse logistics. This enables Auping to reuse the raw materials.

By offering Sleep-As-A-Service, Auping achieves two objectives: sat-isfied customers and a transition to cradle-to-cradle production. The circular economy is probably therefore the main driver for many of its customers to switch to an As-A-Service offer for this bed manu-facturer. (www.auping.com/en/circular)

Hotel chains are naturally a promising target for a bedding manu-facturer because the volumes are large; sales are made in hundreds of units and beds are replaced at a faster rate than in the consumer market.

Most hospitality groups already use a subscription model for their buildings, TV's, bed sheets, towels, telephones, and so on...

However, in this market, beds are still considered a consumable. Regular renewal is attractive from a commercial standpoint but the toll on the environment is high. This is an opportunity for Auping, who aim to transition to cradle-to-cradle production.

As a Frenchman living in the Netherlands, here's one statistic that I find particularly poignant and alarming: if you piled up all the used mattresses discarded in the Netherlands every year, the pile would be as high as the Eiffel Tower!

So what's the solution? Auping retains ownership of the bed, while the hotel takes care of hospitality. Auping ensures that every guest has a relatively new, comfortable bed. They use the term "circular leasing", whereby they retain ownership of the beds and thus the raw materials they're made of.

The courage of circularity

Implementing an As-A-Service model based on circularity is a real challenge because it involves not only rethinking the business model but also the production method. You need to make a product that will last and use raw materials that can go back into the production cycle.

Putting a fully recyclable product on the market can mean higher production costs than what the customer is prepared to pay. Sometimes it takes one or two product rotations before a profit is turned and the return on investment from reusing the raw materials is achieved. Simply put, making a bed using new raw materials each time is more profitable in the short term than making a bed with raw materials from a second-hand bed.

The book *Cradle to Cradle* by William McDonough and Michael Braungart makes this very point, and singles out for praise entrepreneurs like Auping who have had the courage and ambition to profoundly change the way they produce and market their products.

Indeed, more and more consumers and companies are realizing that resources are limited and looking to use products from environmentally responsible companies. As-A-Service is therefore perfectly in keeping with this awareness and market demand, as demonstrated by Auping. An approach like theirs can create value both for your company and for the planet.

Auping's CEO sums up his experience of transforming the company towards a circular business model: "A circular business model teaches you to look at your company in a new way. It imposes other forms of collaboration and innovation. Ultimately, this leads to a sustainable business model that focuses on the environment and meets the wishes of your customer."

This example shows how the motivation behind an As-A-Service offer can vary from project to project. In the case of Auping, the driving force was circularity and the consequent importance of not transferring ownership of the assets to the user, ensuring that the raw materials return to the production cycle.

Financial impacts

Switching to an As-A-Service business model will invariably affect your company's financial situation – which is the main reason why organizations don't do it. Most of the organizations I've advised on this matter have initially been deterred by the financial implications of shifting their business model; they know if they do, the financial profile of the company will change from one fiscal year to the next. Most of the time, they're right: switching to a subscription-based business model has a huge impact on an organization's finance structure, so the decision should not be taken lightly.

I often see companies that start offering their solution in a subscription-based model because of a demand from a major customer, especially when it's a real deal-breaker for the customer in question. Alternatively, they might do it to win a major tender that requires an As-A-Service offer.

These companies start by offering their product and retaining ownership of the assets, while also providing a range of services and charging an all-inclusive monthly subscription – all with their own in-house resources.

The direct consequence is an explosion in the value of the assets on the company's balance sheet, which gives a completely unbalanced financial picture of the organization. The cash needed for the massive upfront investment comes from the company's bank credit lines, which will of course jeopardize their working capital. The solvency and performance risk remains with the organization, thus putting a strain on its financial health, resulting in some difficult meetings with bankers to negotiate an increase in working capital.

I've seen this scenario time and time again. However, there are other ways to address the financial impact of As-A-Service that create value, rather than stress.

Revenue recognition

With a traditional transactional way of offering products, you receive and recognize all the revenue when title is transferred to your customer. You cash in, recognize revenue and margin, and pay your suppliers and costs. With an As-A-Service offer, you have to bank on your customers paying the bill for the services and products delivered every month. In return, you'll have to bear the costs of the solution you deliver; when hardware is involved, the initial upfront investment can be huge. So how can you deal with the substantial upfront investments As-A-Service requires? You won't cash in immediately as there's no transfer of ownership. So how can you manage revenue?

Sell the rental streams

One common practice in As-A-Service is selling your future rental streams to an external party. Once you have your customer's commitment to use the service and product for a certain amount of time, you can predict your future revenues.

Even if your customers don't commit to a certain timeframe and can return the products every month, you can demonstrate the predictability of the terms commonly used, based on the average term of your customers' contracts. While a Swapfiets customer can return their bike at any time, the average duration of a customer commitment is much longer than a month: this can be seen as customer-by-customer or based on the average of your portfolio of customers. This chain of future monthly income is your new gold! This is the predictable aspect of your business model.

You can offer this "secured" future income to external parties at a discount: in other words, you just sell your future rental streams. In return, these external parties - mainly financial institutions - will offer to pay you the value of those rental streams up-front, for a certain price, which is of course below the amount of the sum of the rents. However, even though the value is lower than the rents, it's still worth applying this model. You can even allow for the cost of the sale of future rental streams in the pricing model. In any event, it solves the issue of the upfront cash investment in assets and services. That way, you can cash in based on the present value of your future rental streams.

You can also decide to transfer ownership of the assets to the financial institution; in addition to selling the rental stream, you can offer to sell them the products. This has the advantage of not having the depreciation of the assets on your balance sheet.

When you offer new hardware to your customers, you'll have to buy back the contract and associated assets from the financial institution. Therefore, such financial mechanisms require a certain degree of expertise and experience if they are to be implemented correctly.

Selling future rental streams and transferring ownership are only possible under certain conditions. First of all, your customers have to be sufficiently financially stable to pay the monthly subscription. (Presumably, your financial partners will run credit checks on your customer base.) You may even have to ask for specific securities and guarantees; an obvious one would be simply setting up a direct debit for the monthly subscription fee. The financial party you transfer the rental stream to may ask to handle the collection process itself.

Secondly, there's the issue of performance risk. Who will carry the burden of a defaulting customer if the service is not delivered as expected? It's therefore vital to demonstrate your ability to deliver the service on a continual basis – especially if you don't deliver all the services in-house and use subcontractors. This is one of the key criteria that an external party will analyze when considering buying your future rental streams: performance risk. That is why I've devoted an entire chapter to it.

When to recognize the revenue

Once you've decided to offer your future rental streams to the market, you'll have to make the next decision: when do you book the revenue? As I mentioned earlier, company board members often want to implement this business model because it generates recurring revenue and retains clients.

Selling the future rental streams means you can decide when to recognize revenue. Would you rather book it up-front, as in a transactional business model? You still can. This is what many companies opt for, to avoid a major drop in revenue from one fiscal year to the next. Alternatively, you can choose not to book revenue upfront but on a monthly basis. That way, you get the best of both worlds – you address the cash issue and generate recurring revenue to boot!

Either way, you need to take some time to weigh up the different options with the help of your accountants and external auditors. If your company is listed and it complies with international accounting standards such as IFRS 16, you'll have to spend some time on your revenue recognition strategy.

In addition, let's not forget that once you've moved from a product-based business model to an As-A-Service one, your revenue will become *more* predictable, not less. I'm sure I don't need to explain to any readers the value of a company that can accurately predict the next three years of revenue.

Robots

Robots are no longer just a technology fad but a reality in a number of industries. And now Robots-As-A-Service are here to stay.

Robots have had a lasting impact in the automotive and manufacturing sectors, where they have significantly increased the profitability of the major players for decades. Robotics is now developing rapidly with new use cases in mid-sized companies and in new industry sectors. It is on this wave that a number of new players are developing new offers. As new arrivals have to make a dent in the industry to stand out from the existing players, some, like Locus Robotics (locusrobotics.com) are choosing to offer their solution exclusively in the As-A-Service model.

Locus Robotics is a scale-up company that has developed the "LocusBot" robot, specially designed to work intelligently alongside logisticians in the warehouses. Equipped with sensors, it is capable of routing references across a distribution site after locating them. The employees are then responsible for retrieving the products from the machine's bins. Locus Robotics currently has 4,000 robots deployed across 80 sites. It estimates that in the next few years, the number of customers will increase tenfold, and more than a million warehouse robots will be installed.

The principle of Robots-As-A-Service as applied by Locus Robotics is simple: automated robotic processes combined with a wide range of services, all for a monthly fee.

What is interesting about Locus Robotics is that the solution has been available since 2016 as a Robots-As-A-Service model only, meaning Locus made the ambitious choice to provide its solution on a monthly fee basis only, right from its first customer. This is a great example of new players in an emerging market combining an innovative offering with a subscription-based formula, without ever considering selling their robots. And with good reason: the package, consisting of the robot, the robot fleet management software, the maintenance and and the ongoing updates are a complete, As-A-Service solution; buying the LocusBot would make no sense.

Some people claim that Robots-As-A-Service is the key to the fourth industrial revolution.

Companies of all sizes are interested in using robotics in the As-A-Service model for its flexibility, scalability and much lower entry cost, which is substantially lower than the traditionally high investments in robotics. This broadens the market by allowing small and mid-sized companies to benefit from robotic solutions without having to make a prohibitive initial investment.

Robots are used across a variety of industries ranging from ware-houses to order processing centers, healthcare and security. For example, there are robotics solutions to increase security, with robots patrolling buildings and collecting data, which is then processed by algorithms to improve security operations.

The rapid entry of new robotic solutions in these sectors is possible because Robots As-A-Service lowers the entrance barrier, thereby enabling potential users to test and quickly deploy robotics solutions. As companies that use robotics are generally already at ease with the software As-A-Service business model, it's a natural fit.

The Locus Robotics offer is one example among many in this fast-growing sector. What stands out in all Robots-As-A-Service offers is the complexity of the integration of the product (the robot) with the rest of the solution: fleet management software; data recovery and processing; Artificial Intelligence and the application of algorithms to the data; feedback in the form of a learning machine; the need for quality maintenance to ensure flawless operational continuity, and so on.

The broad scope of the offer makes the provision of a monthly fee an obvious and essential option, which is why new market players are offering their solution exclusively as a monthly subscription model.

Solvency risk

There's a 100% chance one of your customers will not be able to pay the monthly installments because of insolvency. I deal with this problem on a regular basis and my conclusion is always the same: we could have been better prepared.

When designing an As-A-Service offer you always need to ask yourself: why would this customer stop paying? If the answer is because of poor quality of service, see the chapter on performance risk. If the answer is because of malfunction of the assets included in the contract, this has to do with the warranty, and thus the manufacturers of the equipment. If the answer is because the equipment has been damaged, stolen or destroyed by fire or vandalism, this is related to the insurance that you or your customer should have taken out on the assets. Finally, if the answer is because they've run out of funds and can't pay anymore, it's solvency risk.

The implications of an insolvent customer are easy to grasp: you've invested in specific products, or even produced them, to deliver them in an As-A-Service model; you've bought external services such as installation or maintenance; you've acquired software licences to provide the digital part of the experience, and so on. You have an agreement that says the customer will pay you a certain amount per month which covers all those costs and, once they've been paid for, your profit. So, in the unfortunate event that this customer is unable to pay you the monthly installments, you will potentially incur substantial losses.

Unlike a transactional business model, As-A-Service is a long-term engagement with your customer – up to 15 years for Energy-As-A-Service contracts, for example. Therefore any solvency assessment you do at the start of your collaboration may no longer be valid two or three years later.

If you have a business model like Swapfiets, the solvency risk is even higher as you are dealing directly with consumers and can't run a credit check on every single individual.

Best practices for mitigating customer solvency risk

The importance of the choice of asset type, as described in the chapter "What hardware to include", will become evident if and when you reach this unfortunate stage of the customer relationship. When an asset is vital to your customer's core business, they are highly unlikely to stop paying for it. An asset that you can manage remotely will allow you to control your customer's payment behavior. An asset that you can collect means you'll be able to use it for another customer or sell it on the second-hand market.

Even before signing the contract you need to look out for potential warning signs, such as a customer wanting to do a sale and leaseback within two weeks, which would mean that he is craving cash, or asking to spread the contracts over a longer period to reduce the monthly rent. Your sales people won't necessarily be your allies at this stage of the sales process; their goal is to close deals, and as far as they're concerned, customer solvency issues are something for management to worry about, not them.

It is also crucial to estimate your customers' market position and the likelihood of their going bankrupt. Are you dealing with a market leader or an outsider? Is there enough staying power for your customer in its market?

Obviously, running financial checks on your customers is the first step before entering into an As-A-Service contract. There are a number of solutions on the market for doing this and you're probably already familiar with services such as Graydon (www.graydon.nl).

The main difference from a transactional business model is that you will have to work on a much longer term than you are used to, from six months to 15 years, for example.

You may decide to outsource this risk to insurance companies or funders by selling your rental streams and assets as collateral, contract by contract. This means that, against your contracts and assets, the solvency risk will not be yours anymore.

You can also mitigate the risk by reselling your portfolio of customers and rentals to an insurance company and agreeing on a default rate for which you are covered. For example, if less than 5% of the total portfolio is in default, there is no impact on your business and the loss is covered by the insurance company.

What if?

Even if you can outsource this risk, you have to make sure you're ready to address insolvency when it happens. Experience has taught me that no amount of insurance or risk outsourcing can get you out of trouble that easily. Risk bearers will always try to find reasons not to bear the risk, mainly referring to your obligations and, in many cases, identifying a breach of those obligations and therefore a breach of contract. What does being ready mean? It means being able to recoup the amount missing between the upfront investments you've made and the outstanding rentals. Put more simply, on a three-year contract, a customer that stops paying after two years still owes you at least 30% of your investment and your profit!

Before getting into a dispute with customers over payment of rentals in the event of insolvency, I always discuss payment schemes and the possibility of adjusting them to suit the customer's debt profile. You have the flexibility and – to a certain extent – the responsibility to support your customers in difficult times, especially if your solution is vital to their core business.

If the situation deteriorates and all attempts have failed, one way to recoup your investments is by recovering the assets. It's crucial to have legal rights to the assets since it won't always be obvious to an administrator that you're the owner.

These situations will put a lot of stress on your organization. So it's a good idea to have an emergency plan in place. From credit checks to collecting the asset, make sure to incorporate a number of ways to reduce the impact of customer insolvency on your As-A-Service model.

Wine Barrels

Wine barrels have existed for centuries and, unlike the artifacts of the automotive or IT industries, they have not undergone regular innovations. They are thus not the most obvious candidate for a subscription-based model.

However, there is a strong driver for regularly refreshing the asset; the components in oak barrels affect the flavor of the wine, imparting a distinctive wooded note. Oak contains a substance called vanillin, which as its name suggests, gives the wine a subtle, slightly smoky vanilla aroma. This, combined with the tannin of the oak, improves the ageing process. However, the woody taste fades as the barrel ages, meaning the barrels need to be regularly replaced, making them a perfect product to be offered in an As-A-Service solution. At the main wineries, each new vintage is aged half in new barrels, half in used barrels from the previous year. Every year, they renew half of their stock!

One player took the lead on this market, namely H&A Location, who have been successfully running an As-A-Service offer for wine barrels since 2004 (ha-barrelmanagement.com). On their website, they summarize their added value in the wine industry as follows: "From the moment you enter your wine cellar, H&A's professionals will help you manage your barrels by giving them meaning and value".

In 2020, they managed an impressive 750,000 wine barrels, reporting revenue of €320 million. Their customer testimonials are unanimous in their praise of H&A Location's services, stressing that it allows the wineries to focus on their core business: making wine!

Wineries and chateaux are ideal customers when it comes to solvency risk: they're financially solid, with a long track record, and wealthy families own many of them. Owning a *grand cru classé* in the Bordeaux region is the ultimate status symbol for the Fortune 500: it's a guarantee of authenticity and makes you part of history. H&A Location therefore has very little to worry about where customer solvency is concerned. Add to that the importance of wine barrels in a winery's core business and you have the ideal conditions for As-A-Service risk management.

The level of administrative service required for a wine barrel is relatively limited, and involves mostly administrative services such as invoice management, assistance with accounting, inventory of financed barrels, and contract and market statistics.

The main services are delivered at the end of the lifecycle of the barrels; these involve collecting and reselling them on the second-hand market. At this stage, a range of services is delivered, ranging from waterproof testing to disinfection.

The barrels are then sold to smaller wineries or large wine-producing regions such as the Spanish Rioja. Some of the barrels are even sold to Scottish distilleries. "Barrels that have contained Sauternes, for example, are much sought-after for the sweetness they bring. Some whiskeys or rums even mention it on the label," according to H&A Location.

H&A Location is a great example of how a highly stable, centuries-old ownership-driven market can be converted to As-A-Service.

The mechanism is the same as the other offers we've looked at here: H&A retains ownership of the barrels and offers the wineries a range of services enabling them to focus on their core business. The various risks listed in this book – solvency, performance and obsolescence – are obviously simpler to manage in this case, making this market highly scalable.

It's often difficult to identify the favorable conditions for setting up an As-A-Service offer – even when the product or service in question is right under your nose. This is exactly what happened to the founders of H&A Location, who are based in the Bordeaux area. Like Swapfiets, this offer is one of many examples that can inspire you when it comes to identifying a blue ocean in your industry. To do this you need to find an asset that is used daily and could be offered as a comprehensive, all-inclusive subscription package.

The most interesting aspect here is that H&A Location's barrel management offer is the brainchild of entrepreneurs from the ICT leasing industry, not barrel manufacturers. Once again, it's not the manufacturers who are offering their own products via these models; instead, intermediaries are taking the lead.

To go back to the subject of wine, as a European, and in particular, a French national, I can't resist mentioning one nugget of wine trivia. The presence of vanillin in oak may explain why a number of New World wine producers, in the Americas, Australia and New Zealand, for example, add raw or roasted wood chips, shavings, sawdust and the like to their wine, instead of using the traditional barrel, to save time and money on the production process. The use of wood chips in wine production is currently banned in EU member states, but is still authorized in most of the world's other wine-producing countries. Now, who said the French were chauvinistic?

Taking into account the type of equipment and its lifecycle, the customer profile in terms of solvency, and the level of service delivered by a compact ecosystem, it turns out that wine barrels are an ideal market in which to implement an As-A-Service offer.

Performance risk

When you move from providing a product to an As-A-Service solution – including your product of course – the user's expectations of you as a supplier will change radically. This has an important impact on your performance risk.

When you offer a monthly subscription, the user might decide to stop paying the next month if the service doesn't meet expectations.

Performance risk is the risk associated with the services you deliver to the user and their perception of how those services live up to expectations. However excellent the chain of service you deliver is, you're only as strong as the lowest service component of your offer.

Managing expectations

When entering into an As-A-Service offer the supplier makes a commitment to the user: to deliver a solution and an experience that will provide seamless access to a service and associated product.

When manufacturers or distributors make the shift from transferring ownership to offering usership, users have a completely different view of the supplier's obligations. They expect complete outsourcing of the lifecycle of the product and associated services. In short, they expect a solution, not just a product.

Let's take the example of the car-leasing industry. As the happy driver of a car offered as part of an As-A-Service solution, you expect constant access to a range of services to ensure optimal use of your car. For example, you need to be able to fill your tank anytime, anywhere, without having to pay for fuel upfront.

If one morning as you're walking down the street to your car you see there's a broken window, on the very day you have an important business meeting, you expect the car lessor to provide you with a solution to fix the problem asap, which might mean them giving you a replacement car.

Come winter, you'll expect them to supply you with winter tires so you can drive on snowy roads. When you have an accident, you expect them to provide you with a replacement car as soon as possible. When your car needs a service, you expect them to have an agreement with a maintenance provider to arrange this – and so on and so forth. The list is endless.

As an As-A-Service solution supplier, you can decide how many services you want to add to your product to enhance the user experience. Just be careful about what you promise.

We've all had experiences of promises that weren't delivered. I personally hate to be disappointed by a solution for which only the marketing turns out to be solid. If the first steps in a new experience fall short of expectations, the whole experience will fail.

Today's users are accustomed to solutions that work, often involving a digital interaction with their smartphone. They want it to work immediately, without having to read an instruction manual. And when the solution goes wrong, it has to be up and running again quickly and easily.

In the previous example of Classroom-As-A-Service, the users – the students and teachers – expect continuous access to the platform and thus an enjoyable, seamless e-learning experience. If any part of the solution stops performing, the whole experience is ruined. What if the Wi-Fi isn't working? What if the e-learning software is slow one day? What if a child knocks their tablet off the desk and breaks the screen? In all these scenarios, the school will expect continuity of service (with no change in the monthly subscription fee, naturally!)

With Swapfiets, the "Amsterdammer" using the service expects their bike to be constantly operational so they can get to their business meeting, dinner with friends or yoga lesson – even if there's a flat tire.

Under promise, over deliver

Managing users' expectations is key. What are you really offering them? Where does your service start and end? What specific situations do you cover? And are these scenarios included in the subscription fee?

It's vital to set clear boundaries so that the user knows exactly what to expect. The more precisely the services are described and understood by both supplier and user, the more closely you'll meet expectations.

I would even advise under-promising and over-delivering, by offering faster services or services that go one step beyond whatever was stipulated in the contract.

As you're not being paid upfront for the transfer of ownership but instead paid on a regular basis, your main goal should be to keep the user satisfied throughout the journey, at every touch point of the service you provide. An unsatisfied user will simply stop paying the supplier – and give them a bad rating on social media. You can mitigate this risk with specific clauses in your subscription contract. But ultimately, you will have to handle it.

Performance risk management: in-house or with partners?

We have seen the different models for delivering the service in previous chapters. At one end of the spectrum, everything is done in-house, with your own teams and resources. At the other end of the spectrum, everything is outsourced to specialists. The model you choose will affect your performance risk.

By providing the complete solution in-house, you can mitigate performance risk, since you have a grip on all the parameters of the service. Of course, the downside is that you won't have the expertise for all the services you deliver, which means you'll be limited in terms of the experience you can provide to the user.

In the case of Classroom-As-A-Service, for example, Econocom could never have provided e-learning software. However, by joining forces with a software company, we were able to expand the scope of service – which also meant increasing performance risk.

The opposite of in-house is outsourcing your services, by teaming up with partners that specialize in the type of services you want to deliver. In this case, the scope of services is endless: the only limit is your imagination.

The challenge will be monitoring all the suppliers' ability to understand your offer and deliver it just the way you would. The user experience has to be a single, holistic one, not a mishmash of different services and company cultures.

Working with partners makes managing quality of service more complex – meaning performance risk is higher – but it also improves the experience of the end user.

Solvency and performance risk go hand in hand

Earlier, we looked at the financial impact of converting your business to As-A-Service, particularly with respect to mitigating the solvency risk. Any third party you partner with to get the solvency risk off your books will also pay attention to the performance risk.

You'll have to decide whether you also want to transfer performance risk to an external party. In other words, you can reach solutions where you also outsource the performance risk together with the solvency risk.

The better you manage your performance risk, the easier it will be to outsource all the risks and get the future revenue streams pre-financed. The way to make this happen is either by having a maximum number of services delivered in-house or by teaming up with other parties with a solid track record for delivering the relevant service.

To keep your customers happy, have satisfied users and be able to pre-finance future revenues, it's crucial to focus on addressing performance risk so your new business model isn't under pressure and is scalable.

Finding your blue ocean

It's time to draft a business plan to confirm your assumptions and get traction from your teams and ecosystem.

It is good to get used to the rationale of deciding which offer will work. I have often been in the position of deciding where to allocate resources to offer a complete As-A-Service solution and I have tried to share my "train of thought" here.

With this book in your hand, you now have all the information and examples you need to create your own decision matrix.

So lets design your offer step by step

1. **Identify a need requiring different services that are complicated and time-consuming for a customer/user to organize.**
To get the full experience of this solution or product, the user has to deal with a fragmented, uncoordinated service provider that they have to assess and address themselves.

2. **What services can you include in the offer that are already available on the market but provided by different sources or parties?**
Take the example of Swapfiets: as a consumer I can buy a bike, fix a flat tire, get insurance to replace it if it's stolen, and go to a bike shop once a year to have it serviced. All Swapfiets does is combine services that are already available separately into a single package.

3. **Identify service providers in your market**
Who are the are best in class in their field, and offer all these services as a single package.

4. **Choose between delivering services in-house or via partnerships.**
Will you deliver everything on your own or team up with partners that are already strong in their market? In the case of Leaseplan, joining forces with Carglass to fix broken windows brought consid-

erable added value to the driver. Would Carglass have been the entry point for Cars-As-A-Service?

5. Spot the main hardware type that is key in your industry and work around it.

What are the main cash-register systems in supermarkets? What's the biggest brand of screens in airports? Which household appliances are the most time-consuming and require the most services? Coffee machines? Clothes? Gardens? Shaving kits?

6. Decide which hardware/products to include in the offer.

Will it be mobile? Remotely controlled? Will it meet all the criteria listed in the chapter "which hardware to include"?

7. Check if you can switch service or product providers if needed.

Teaming up with suppliers who have a monopoly in your market will make you dangerously dependent on them.

8. Look at the history of technological obsolescence risk in your industry and the expected life cycle of the solution you are offering.

121

Will you provide a solution that uses a brand new technology or would you rather go for a more stable, mature solution? Look at manufacturers' product roadmaps and make your decisions with this in mind. I strongly recommend you have an in-house team in charge of global technology monitoring so you can keep abreast of any new trends and major shifts in your market.

9. Address the solvency risk.

Is your target customer solvent, or do they have a high-risk profile? Offering a solution to state schools or hospitals rather than to private individuals or mid-sized companies in the private sector, will have considerable implications in terms of solvency. The lower the solvency risk, the faster you will grow your business.

10. Prepare for your arrival on the second-hand market.

Are you prepared to own a large fleet of assets and manage their second life? Which second-hand market will you easily be able to access when the equipment is returned at the end of the contract? Will you be able to coexist with the manufacturers in this market – or will they see you as a threat because you're supplying second-hand products to rival their new offers?

11. Prepare upsales by validating how to monetize a community.

Can you collect data and thus gain valuable insights into customer behavior and enhance the user experience? If the answer is yes, with your users' consent you can attract new service providers by working together on a joint database. Can you provide more services during the contract term while generating upsales?

12. Determine what your customer's As-A-Service needs are.

Are they looking for the freedom to stop the contract every month or will they be able to commit to a long-term contract such as three to five years?

As an illustration of the points above, if you offer Washing Machines-As-A-Service to hospitals and gather data on rates of use, you can then approach laundry suppliers and include them in your offer. With some smart negotiating, you should be able to get some back margins or introduction fees and thus lower your subscription fee for the washing machine. You could even consider offering the washing machine for a much lower monthly amount than the purchase price if the user opts for the associated services. This is how printer suppliers work: the printers themselves cost very little, so they make their profit from selling ink cartridges. The same principle can be applied to an As-A-Service offer.

Now you have a more complete picture of the areas you need to focus on, let's go back to the example of Classroom-As-A-Service that we discussed earlier.

The rationale behind this offer was that e-learning is growing, yet the rate of use of this type of software is still very low due to infrastructure issues. The problem with implementing this solution is that it involves managing hardware to make it run smoothly. Schools don't have an IT department to handle the implementation and lifecycle of the devices. The customers are schools with a good credit rating, so solvency risk is low. The devices are easy to maintain since these are mainly tablets and they can therefore be swapped in the event of maintenance or damage. The software vendor chosen has a good track record, so performance risk is pretty low. The market value of the devices will remain high in the event of an early return as we go with the leading brands. The service can be discontinued remotely. The price we can offer is the going rate.

The choice of go-to-market was made by making an assessment using the twelve steps model outlined above.

Once you've made your choices, identified the blue ocean in your industry sector, identified your business model and had it approved by your board, it's a race against time. Your main challenge at this stage of your offer is to build a wide installed base as quickly as possible.

Being the owner of a large installed base and obtaining a significant number of users as quickly as possible will enable you to get a foothold in your market and ecosystem. The race for the installed base is the key to mastering the offer in your market and achieving economies of scale within two to three years. Above all, it will secure your future by making you competitor-proof.

Find your blue ocean

You need to be constantly open to spotting the areas where there is space for an As-A-Service offer. Let me share an example from my personal life.

One of the things I love about Amsterdam is sailing on the canals with friends on a lovely summer day. You don't need to be an expert sailor; the boats are basically floating café terraces. So one of the few things that I own is a boat, which is moored near my house.

I thought long and hard before deciding to buy: I was somewhat daunted by the prospect of having to manage all the service providers required to deliver the perfect experience. I decided to team up with a couple of neighbors to buy a boat, and share the costs and maintenance. We went for an aluminum hull to keep maintenance costs down and an electric engine to ensure minimal maintenance. This also enabled us to comply with a new regulation in the city of Amsterdam whereby, in five years' time, only electric boats will be allowed.

Despite all the sensible, logical reasoning that led me to choose this particular model of boat and opt for co-ownership, thereby reducing the hassle of ownership to a minimum, I still dream of being able to take out a subscription that would allow me to use a boat with my friends and family, with maximum enjoyment and minimum hassle.

124 It's not just about wanting to avoid wasting time and energy on running and managing the asset; I also want to keep my mind free to focus on things that are important and valuable to me, rather than worrying about problems that could arise when using the boat.

I did look for a solution to sale the canals, a Boat-As-A-Service solution, but never found one...

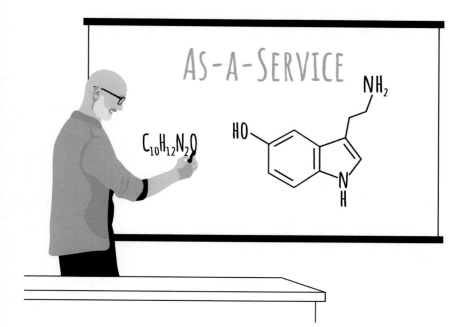

Pleasure versus happiness: the sales force dilemma

A number of studies have been conducted on the difference between pleasure and happiness, the first being something that is based in the short term, while the latter is based in the long term.

I have dedicated some time and headspace to grasping the difference between the two concepts. The rise of social media, with its promise of instant rewards, has recently driven home to me how dependent modern-day man is on pleasure. I've seen how my kids are drawn to these platforms and how the features developed by the main social media players maintain this addiction to pleasure. There is even evidence of an actual chemical process that is triggered by the pursuit of instant gratification, pleasure being related to dopamine while happiness is related to serotonin.

What if we use these lessons to better understand the hurdles in the shift from a transactional business model – which yields instant gratification – to a subscription-based model, which brings long-term satisfaction?

A salesforce used to selling transactional contracts has to focus on delivering "pleasure" to management: instant rewards, short-term successes, simplified sales processes, and short-term decision-making.

An As-A-Service business model, on the other hand, is closer to the concept of "happiness" as it's about the long term, it benefits more people, it is the result of teamwork, and it is recurring.

So the question is, how can you get your sales force – and your whole organization – to shift from a dopamine mindset to a serotonin mindset; from 'pleasure' to 'happiness'?

Cultural shift

When implementing an As-A-Service strategy, you need to be aware of the cultural shift this will bring about within an organization. Aside from the impacts we have already looked at in previous chapters, you also need to consider the marketing and sales aspects of this new go-to-market strategy. I've frequently seen the disparity between C-level's naive enthusiasm about launching new business models and sales' extreme reluctance to make the switch.

For decades, your customers and sales teams have been used to the principle of transferring ownership of your products; selling extra services such as maintenance is already a struggle for many organizations.

Adding a recurring income stream to a product by selling an associated maintenance contract has been the Holy Grail for a number of product-based businesses over the years; making sure the sales force includes it in their basic offer, however, is a whole other ball game.

Initiatives such as sales challenges, incentives and bonus schemes are often implemented to try to get sales to upsell – with varying degrees of success. But what if the whole pricing model is based on a monthly fee? Will your sales team make the transition easily? Always bear in mind that a transactional business model involves a much shorter, simpler sales process than a usership model.

129

Change management

Entering a subscription model requires much closer attention to the sales process: it involves longer sales cycles, more people in the process, more complex legal work, longer negotiations, and objections that are difficult to answer due to the salesperson's lack of knowledge on the matter. In fact, you're not actually selling a product anymore: you're selling an experience. This means the account managers in charge of selling this experience have to believe in it, to live and breathe it, and to experience it first-hand. They have to have faith in your company's ability to deliver on the promise you're selling because they are the ones who will have to deal with any issues that arise.

The sales cycle takes longer, and the associated services are more complex. The same goes for the customer: the new solution will take some time to get their heads around, raising new questions, requiring different booking methodologies, and involving different budget lines. They will see it as a black box.

Time and again I've seen that the shift to As-A-Service is clear to management, but when it comes to explaining it in concrete terms to customers, it's much more complex.

Basically, there's a good chance that your As-A-Service offer will end up being a great marketing tool to help you stand out from the competition, but most of your transactions will remain as they are. Your commitment to your shareholders of 50% recurring revenue in three years might come to nothing. Why is that?

Consider these facts: revenue recognition will change; you'll have to address a number of new risks; you'll get a firmer hold on your customers; you'll disrupt the market; you'll create new business models. Then there are all the other things that come under the 'O' of your SWOT analysis – these are all light years away from the concerns of an account manager who's used to reaching monthly targets with transactional business models.

There are many hurdles to overcome, from both the sales and customer perspective. Just because you, the head of a company, are convinced that this is the way forward, it doesn't mean your sales force and customers are. A company's strategy must be easily understood through the sales plan and bonuses of the sales force.

Excuses

Here are some of the things you'll hear from your sales teams: it will save you a lot of time and make things much easier for you if you read them here now rather than having to deal with them in real life. "My customer had some leftover budget to spend this year so it was just easier to close a transactional deal."

"My customer doesn't want to have to bring in the Finance Director to explain a whole new concept; plus, they can't engage the company for more than 12 months, so I decided to sign this deal the usual way for now, and we'll see for the next one."

"My customer has added up the rentals and realized it will work out cheaper to fund the solution themselves."

"My customer is cash-rich and is offended when we offer them a monthly payment scheme."

"My customer doesn't want us to retain ownership of the assets because, if we go bankrupt, they'll lose the assets and will have to find a new supplier."

"My customer wants the freedom to keep the assets for longer than our contract allows."

"My customer receives subsidies so can't use a subscription model."

131

"I need to get Pre-sales onboard to explain all the associated services, but my customer is ready to sign today."

I've seen situations like these hundreds of times – but each time, there is at least one consolation: the sales department are doing their job properly, i.e. trying to generate short-term turnover and business for the company.

To cut a long story short, your company culture could work against your strategy!

The solution: start with an existing customer

The successful recipes I have implemented involve focusing on an existing customer. You'll be able to land your first As-A-Service contract with a customer that knows your organization, knows your services and has years of experience with your products. A customer that sees you as a trusted partner to help reach their strategic goals.

A first deal such as this could happen at C-level, possibly without involving your sales team at all. You'll be given much more credit in your organization when management closes the first deals. However, this shouldn't be the case for more than two or three deals as you'll run the risk of cutting out your sales team and giving the impression that this new model is only a C-level matter.

To move towards a usership-based solution for your customer base, I recommend you follow these two guidelines:
Make the difficult decision of dedicating a specialist sales force. It could be either a direct sales force or pre-sales team in charge of supporting your existing sales force. Either way, my experience has taught me that in-house sales teams need help selling an As-A-Service solution.
Remember the KISS principle: Keep It Short and Simple. Even though the offer requires a complete shift in the way you deliver your products, what's happening in the kitchen has to stay in the kitchen; a seamless experience starts with a seamless offer. We're often so proud of the changes we've implemented that we're tempted to explain them to our customers. However, just ask yourself whether you know exactly how Netflix provides all those movies at your fingertips. What's their IT infrastructure? How do they manage copyright, how can the bandwidth remain stable throughout the movie, and so on. Sure, you need to be ready to answer these questions if they are asked – but don't make them your sales pitch.

Happiness

So where does the happiness part of the As-A-Service business model kick in?

The good news is you'll only have to deal with the complexity of the sales process once. Once you've succeeded in bringing your customer round to the usership model, they are in for the long haul.

The biggest part of the sales effort is the shift from one model to another. However, once you've initiated the usership collaboration, the next deal will be easy to close, as it will come under the umbrella of this new model. In my experience, once customers try usership they rarely go back to a transactional business model. And why would they? Would you go back to DVDs now you've discovered streaming?

A personal example: my hoover broke down recently; it was a year old. Three weeks later, I still hadn't fixed it. What was wrong with it? Could it be repaired? How and where should I fix it? Was the warranty still valid? I really didn't have time for this. I ended up buying a new one... If only my hoover was part of an As-A-Service package and I could sort this out with a simple call or WhatsApp message to my service provider. Mr. Hoover-As-A-Service – meet your first customer!

From linear
to circular
economy

Congratulations: within three years of reading this book you'll be the owner of a large fleet of devices! And if you've offered three-year contracts to your users, you'll start to get those devices back soon...

You've reached a new milestone in your entrepreneurial journey. Until now, you were used to transferring ownership to the user and consequently never seeing the equipment that you had delivered years earlier again. You've never had to worry about managing the second life, recycling the equipment and so forth.

We are all used to the linear economic model. We produce or distribute goods, transfer ownership to our customers, recognize revenue and then start marketing the next version of the product, so we can reproduce this cycle as quickly as possible without thinking or anticipating the end-of-life of this product.

This is the root of the concept of planned obsolescence. You may have heard of the Lightbulb Conspiracy. Over the course of decades, lightbulb manufacturers have deliberately lowered the lifespan of light bulbs gradually. The industry standard of 2,500 hours in 1924 would eventually drop to 1,000 hours by 1940. Lightbulbs were deliberately made more fragile, and competitors would be closely monitored (and if necessary, fined) to ensure strict adherence to product degradation.

We now realize that this economic model has reached its limits and that the natural resources to sustain this approach are slowly but surely disappearing.

The willingness to move to a circular economic model is there but it sometimes seems impossible to achieve. I have had countless discussions with manufacturers of IT devices on this subject. How can a manufacturer change their model by being responsible for the total lifecycle of the goods produced? How do you design production in a way that the goods will be back in the production process in a few years so the natural resources are only used once? How do you ensure the production costs of the first generation of recyclable goods are in line with the market?

According to the Dutch architect Thomas Rau, a product that arrives at the end of its useful life loses its identity (www.rau.eu). An old car that reaches the junkyard has lost its identity either because it can no longer be used, or it is worth nothing.

But what if the car, or any other device, remained the property of the entrepreneur who produced it? The product would never lose its identity. At the end of its useful life, the product would remain a great source of resources from which to produce new ones and the manufacturer who owned it would dedicate resources to getting it back.

Manufacturers are often trapped in their existing economic model, particularly due to the thorny issue of revenue recognition: switching from transfer of ownership to transfer of use invariably disrupts revenue recognition. You can't simply divide your turnover by three or five overnight when entering into a subscription model. How will your shareholders react? And what about share price, if you're a listed company?

I am convinced that entrepreneurs who use the As-A-Service model, including hardware, will be the pioneers of the circular economy. Manufacturers can find a solution in the subscription model of offering usership instead of ownership, and thereby retain ownership of the equipment they produce. Thus, their stock of raw materials will no longer be in the ground but in the products they make available to their users, which they will one day see again.

A strong partnership between an As-A-Service provider and the product manufacturers is the next step. Imagine Swapfiets teaming up with a major bike manufacturer and making these statements: I'll buy your bicycles so you can transfer the ownership to me; I'll provide usership to thousands of cyclists, and after a certain amount of time or number of kilometers, I'll get the bikes back. That way, you'll be sure the bikes are integrated into your production process and I'll commit to buying the new bikes from you.

Such a scenario might seem naive: I've met plenty of manufacturers who dream of subscription models, switching to usership and circular management of their production process. However, I've yet to see one that has taken the plunge!

I truly believe that the concentration of ownership of devices by the As-A-Service providers – as opposed to the current trend, whereby devices are owned by a variety of different players – would be a game-changer.

I'd like to conclude by saying this to As-A-Service entrepreneurs: you'll soon be the proud owner of a large number of devices; you'll have the responsibility of understanding their production and recycling process; you'll have enough economic clout to start getting manufacturers to make the move and you'll be able to offer a usership model on a silver platter to the manufacturers with whom you do business. You'll thus open the door to the circular economy by resolving many of their issues.

138 As-A-Service is therefore one of the routes into a circular economic model. Those new business models will generate new – even better – revenue streams, while contributing to the circular economy shift.

Life-As-A-Service

Anyone who loves sailing as much as I do knows that leaving the shore, even for a few hours, is a way of switching off and freeing your mind. Over the years, sailing provided me with many insights. I would like to share one of them with you, as it's particularly relevant to the subject of this book. I discovered the profound satisfaction of having only a few possessions and therefore satisfying myself through experiences and not belongings.

For years I stuck to coastal navigation. In other words, I used to return to shore every evening, moor in a port or a cove, and spend the night safely and unadventurously. My experience of sailing, of life at sea, was therefore limited to a few hours at a time. Like any sailor, I used to dream of the open seas, of offshore navigation, thinking wistfully of that 360° horizon feeling, with only the sun, the stars and the moon (and a GPS) to guide me; a prospect which both attracted and terrified me.

By a happy combination of circumstances, when I turned 45, I got an invitation to embark on a four-week transatlantic crossing. I took on the challenge. This experience at sea gave me a wealth of insights, which eventually led me to overcome many limiting beliefs and make radical changes in my life.

After just a few days at sea, I realized I could embrace the world I was living in with a single glance. All I had to do was stand at the back of the boat and see that the boat represented a limited space containing all the resources and goods I needed to make this journey, to reach my goal.

French writer Sylvain Tesson describes a similar experience in his account of spending six months in a hut in Siberia: "To live in a folded up space that the eye embraces, that a look allows you to circumscribe and that the spirit represents itself".

The sailing experience forced me to think hard about my life. I had naturally accumulated a lot of stuff, filling a large house from cellar to attic – not to mention the garage and the garden shed. I never thought about it. I was so caught up in the race for more possessions. There, at sea, I realized that throughout my entire life I had been expressing my identity through my belongings.

The conclusion came naturally: the time, energy and headspace I devoted to keeping all these possessions in good working order had far outweighed the pleasure I got from them. As I look back now, I see that the time and energy devoted to those goods was a great way of diverting my mind from the things that really mattered. Every day I see how people – entire families – focus on the logistics of their lives to avoid the most beautiful – and frightening – endless journey: the inner journey, which consists of accumulating experiences, not possessions.

My time is precious, and, after crossing the Ocean, I made the bold decision to live by different principles when I came back ashore on the other side of the Atlantic. The resources and goods I had must be limited to what I needed to achieve my goals: no less, no more. And if my objectives changed, my resources and assets needed to be scaled up or down accordingly.

143

Once back on terra firma, however, the epiphany I had experienced during the Atlantic crossing, this constant search for a balance between the desired experiences and the stuff you need to achieve them, soon just seemed like a beautiful but unattainable vision. Actually putting it into practice seemed so complex to me that I almost dismissed it as a pipe dream.

Radically changing your way of life, getting rid of old habits and things you have accumulated, seemed too difficult to implement. There's peer pressure, the need to 'keep up with the Joneses', and, more importantly, there seemed to be no alternative. There were no precedents, no examples to inspire me. I couldn't make the transition between my aspirations and reality. So I chose to flee, trying to cast a veil over these beautiful prospects, satisfying myself with excesses of all kinds.

But I never forgot that light and free feeling I had on the boat. A seed had been planted. I started to notice things. Did you know, for example, that the average sailing time of a privately owned sailboat is only about two weeks a year? So why own a boat?

I became aware that all the things we own, actually own us, and they have a firm grip on our time and headspace. From a smart TV to a lawn-mowing robot, you need to become an expert in all these fields to understand how to get the best out of the equipment – which, of course, is impossible. So what happens? You spend your time juggling dozens of providers, help desks, support lines, reading manuals and user guides, returning goods to the shops, buying spare parts, making appointments at the weekend to get them fixed, specializing in dozens of disciplines from Wi-Fi to boat's engines – just to make sure everything works when you need it.

And that's assuming you can find the time to use them. I often heard friends say they prefer to go away for their holidays, because if they stayed at home they'd spend all their free time fixing all the things that need to be fixed. Does that sound familiar?

So what's the point of owning things? Why not just use them? Why should the producer of those goods transfer ownership to me, and along with it, the burden of maintaining those goods in perfect working order, of ensuring them, and of future-proofing them? And what if I only need to use them for a limited amount of time?

Then I met a person who actually already lived by the principle I had been contemplating. Esther Jacobs, The Netherlands' first "digital nomad", had no fixed place to live, but traveled the world in total freedom (www.estherjacobs.info). All her possessions fit in one suitcase. Instead of renting a house, the "No Excuses Lady" stays in Airbnb properties, enjoying different locations, lower expenses and the services that come with this arrangement. She never has to clean or maintain her house and a working Wi-Fi connection is the responsibility of the owner of the Airbnb. In fact, she lives "Life As-A-Service"! That freedom inspired me to finally put into practice the insights I had acquired during my crossing.

Esther, who has since become my partner in life, also introduced me to a network of location-independent entrepreneurs, confirming that what I had dreamed of really is possible (www.tropicalmba.com/join-the-dynamite-circle).

I decided to downsize: I went from a 300m2 house to a 30m² apartment. The only possessions I've kept are the ones I really use and enjoy owning the most. I decided to go for quality and not quantity: good clothes, a superb computer, good speakers and some quality furniture.

I am finding more and more ways to just enjoy what I need with no hassle. I got rid of my car and I only use Uber, car sharing and public transport. I rent boats all over the world via a similar sharing service. I got rid of my skiing gear and I enjoy renting the perfectly serviced and brand new material that is available when I go skiing. I've even said goodbye to a coffee machine; instead, I go down the street and enjoy the local coffee shops wherever I happen to be living and have a new experience every time. Just using, not owning, is both satisfying and liberating.

145

The time I have freed up in this way and the mental space I've created, allows me to focus on doing things that give me the most satisfaction: sport, meditation, music, my business, travelling with my grown up children. I have discovered how amazing and satisfying it is to live more simply.

It's not just about the way scaling back on your possessions can make you feel and the brain space it frees up. What I like most about living with fewer possessions is that I travel a lot more. As a result, not being attached to things I own has opened the door to remote work and life, and thus not being dependent on a specific location. When you just use, you can use anywhere on earth!

With more time to live how I want to live, I actually achieve my professional and personal goals faster than I used to, thanks to the reduction of my possessions and the access to more goods in an As-A-Service model. And since I don't own my stuff, I have access to much more experiences than before. Any time I decide to go for a new experience, I always make sure it doesn't entail owning anything.

Don't get me wrong: I'm not against the consumer society that we live in. I'm simply advocating a shift from ownership to usership by promoting As-A-Service models and applying it to my daily life. This benefits the end user, who can focus on enjoying experiences, and the manufacturer, who will improve customer retention and build lasting ties. Finally, it will benefit society as a whole as it opens the door to concentrated ownership, which in turn promotes the circular economy and ways of preserving our precious, limited resources.

There's a major shift in society from focusing on what you have, to what you can experience. Value is not created by possession, but by gaining experiences that no one can ever take away from you. The magic happens when you crave more headspace and less stuff because you realize it is stopping you from really enjoying your life. When you decide to move from possession to use, you not only reduce the number of things you own but you also change your perspective of what you value and prioritize in your life. Through this process, you'll see that not only will you save time and money, but you'll also embrace a whole new way of thinking.

Of course, all these principles also apply to the B2B world. Using instead of owning enables your organization and your customers to focus on their core business and to have time and resources to focus on their goals, just as I made this move to focus on the core of my own life. I am curious how you will apply this in your life and business.

Avoid these commonly made mistakes

The demand for As-A-Service is growing stronger every day and rapidly spreading from the B2C to the B2B markets. Manufacturers and service integrators are being pushed by their customers and shareholders to offer new consumption models that focus on use rather than ownership.

If you plan to get in on this market, great – just be aware that the road to success is bumpy and full of potholes. In my time I've seen plenty of As-A-Service ventures fail, for a variety of reasons that I will discuss below.

The change curve is steep and the challenges should not be underestimated. It's like a mountain hike that looks easy in the guidebook, but turns out to be much more difficult by the time you've been climbing for four hours. It is advisable to have an experienced guide with you when you explore unknown territories.

Commonly made mistakes

In my 25 years in the business, during which I have been involved in hundreds of attempted cases or existing programs, I have been witness to the fact that, no matter what the industry is, the same mistakes are often repeated. There is a lot of enthusiasm and will to develop this new model and to win the first customers, but the project backfires because of these mistakes, which could have been avoided. To avoid killing the energy of the team involved, here is a list of the most commonly made mistakes. My aim is to ensure that your As-A-Service journey can preserve the speed and energy needed to succeed.

Not taking enough time

Just sign up for a Google As-A-Service notification and you'll get loads of email articles on topics such as Mobility-As-A-Service, Aircraft-As-A-Service, and so on. In just a few months since I started writing this book, a significant number of offers have come onto the market. While they appear new, these models were actually launched three to five years ago; they take time to get off the ground. Take at least six months to design your program and prepare for 18 to 24 months of implementation.

Not onboarding the specific skills required

It's challenging to have a product as part of an As-A-Service package, because this requires specific skills. Aside from the usual issues associated with implementing new business models, such as marketing and changing the sales culture, you also need to master financial engineering in order to ensure the feasibility and durability of the offers, while at the same time making the model appeal to users and shareholders alike. The right skills are needed to move forward as well as privileged "plug and play" collaborators who have already won the As-A-Service T-shirt many times in their race for the installed base.

Implementation methodology being too standard

The concept of As-A-Service itself isn't new, but it is being applied to new industries outside IT. The standard implementation methodology can be easily replicated. But will it work for your model? It takes time to conduct a deep analysis of the readiness of the ecosystem involved around your new offer. There is no "one size fits all"!

Forgetting the change management aspects

I can give you plenty of examples of organizations that start their As-A-Service journey by using their in-house resources and getting a handful of managers to oversee it, without taking into account the inevitable issue of resistance to change. It is therefore essential that the organization's C-suite engages its employees as well as the ecosystem and conveys its vision to them.

Lacking inspiration

When you begin this journey, you'll be taking a lot of your internal and external stakeholders out of their comfort zone. And it will be two to three years before you start reaping the benefits of the recurring business model you're putting in place. Over time, the effort-reward ratio will improve. The road to As-A-Service is long and you constantly need to inspire your team and ecosystem, and remind them why you're doing it in order to keep them engaged.

Offers not being clearly defined. If you leave room for interpretation by your sales team or customers, every transaction will become unique and thus challenging to manage in the future. The standardisation of your offers and contracts is key to scaling up your As-A-Service model.

Not integrating enough services

If your customers still have to arrange some services themselves, your offer will be only half finished. Providing an offer that does not cover the complete set of needs will leave room for your customer to find reasons not to choose this new model.

Not having good back-to-back contracts with your suppliers that enable the As-A-Service solution

When your ecosystem is not clearly onboarded, your performance risk will increase, which will limit your ability to find capital and therefore to scale your new offer.

Using the same sales force as the one you were used to

A sales team that is used to transactional business will have major challenges in moving to an As-A-Service offer. Such an offer needs to be approached with strong consultative selling skills, very often addressing the C-suite of your customers and prospects.

Addressing the customer the same way when onboarding and renewing the subscription

Signing the first As-A-Service transaction and renewing an existing contract are as different as hunting and farming. The sales process cannot be compared to refreshing existing customers so it should therefore be handled by two different types of sales profiles.

Not creating incentives for the salesforce or management

The horizon and targets of the salesforce rarely extend beyond the current quarter, whereas the benefits and return of As-A-Service will take two to three years to kick in. Even if it is obvious for the management to go for As-A-Service, the sales team won't focus on the new offers if they are not rewarded for selling them.

Weakening your balance sheet

If the need for cash plus the solvency risk are not outsourced, the capital needed will be huge and the risks will be high. You can start your As-A-Service journey by using your own balance, but, after a few new As-A-Service customers – some of whom will present solvency issues – the scalability of the model will be compromised.

Depending too much on leasing companies for the refinancing

The leasing companies are an important component of your ability to deliver the offer, but if you let them lead, the customer experience will be down to hardware leasing.

Stopping developing the offer

Each stage of the As-A-Service offer has its own challenges. Even organizations that have already implemented a solution will encounter new challenges every day. You should never stop improving and adding value. For example building a real As-A-Service offering that allows the client to recognize the contract in Opex under IFRS, as the client can bring the partnership to an end at any time.

Need help on your As-A-Service journey?

Because of the many requests for help to get started with, or improve existing As-A-Service offers, I decided to set up a company to share my expertise. My team and I at Black Winch B.V. help companies turn their traditional business model into a scalable subscription model, i.e. an As-A-Service package, with the product included.

Whether it's assessing the potential and feasibility of bringing an As-A-Service product to market, or improving the profitability of an existing solution, we offer a wide range of expertise to help clients and shareholders achieve their strategic goals with As-A-Service solutions.

As we know there's no "one size fits all" approach, Black Winch helps organizations to create or optimize their As-A-Service business model by providing expertise in areas from defining your strategy, to the incubation stage and generating synergies with existing models.

We truly believe that As-A-Service is one of the ways to achieve a circular business model. These new business models will generate new, improved revenue streams, while helping the transition to the circular economy. And that's also why we do what we do!

We've paved the way, covering eight areas to help you implement a scalable As-A-Service business model.

1. Audit
One of the points we will address with the audit is the eligibility of the product that is part of your As-A-Service offering. It has to fulfil certain criteria in order to mitigate risk, deliver a flawless, innovative user experience and generate new types of revenue beyond what you typically earn from your services.

2. Strategy
Part of the strategic advice will focus on the question of how to create shareholder value by accelerating the refreshing rate of your products and therefore generating predictable recurring revenues. Once we've found your blue ocean, it's time to write a business plan to validate your assumptions, get buy-in from your teams and ecosystem, and get your first wins.

155

3. Marketing
Spreading the word to the market is key; this has to be achieved in a more comprehensive way than by just adding an extra layer to your existing offers.

4. Sales
Together with the sales teams, we build different financial and technical refresh scenarios in order to optimize the customer experience.

5. Back office
The added value we provide by focusing on back office activity is designed to create the discipline to industrialize offers and therefore processes in order to scale and facilitate the sales journey.

6. Funding

On aspects of funding, we will support the implementation of a strategy to access funds in order to provide cash flows and light up the balance sheet. The financial impact in terms of cash consumption, revenue recognition and solvency risks is an area where you need expertise to find solutions to make it scalable.

7. Finance

The revenue recognition analysis with the finance team will make sure that your new business model enables growth. We will also help you to mitigate risks such as solvency, performance and technological obsolescence.

8. Suppliers

In order to onboard your ecosystem, we align supplier SLAs with the As-A-Service contract and validate your operational capability to deliver the in-house services. When you're used to a transactional business model, i.e. selling a product and transferring ownership, you sometimes need an outsider to suggest what services could be offered with your product.

Black Winch has achieved its goal when your As-A-Service business model has been successfully and sustainably implemented. We'll help you every step of the way to secure this new business model and satisfy your customers and shareholders.

Whether you're a first-timer or want to further develop an existing As-A-Service solution, you can step into our implementation process at any stage.

And, naturally, we offer our service As-A-Service! For a fixed monthly amount, you'll get all the support you need to implement this new model or improve an existing one.

Last but not least, we are proud to have a hands-on approach, in which each step of our methodology comes with a concrete result. That's our commitment to your success.

From a buzzword to a concrete model. Are you going to wait for your customers to use a rival As-A-Service solution? Or are you daring enough to seize this opportunity today?

If you want proven success models and expert advice, we at Black Winch are happy to help. Reach out at **Blackwinch.eu** for a free consultation.

Acknowledgements

I am very grateful to Esther Jacobs, my partner, who helped me bring this work to life. Her 'Reverse Writing methodology' gave me a step-by-step path, starting with the back then front cover, continuing with the table of contents, and on to the book you now hold in your hands. I wrote most of it during two of her writing retreats (in Thailand and Mallorca) and I finished it because of her tireless encouragement to "get it done". All this has allowed me to experience and complete this adventure. If you are thinking about writing a book, I can only recommend her services (www.reversewriting.com).

The holistic vision of a society based exclusively on a subscription model is a perspective that I thank Joseph Pulicano for sharing with us in the foreword to this book. I would like to thank him for taking the time to shed additional light on the As-A-Service impacts on our daily lives as consumer or businesses managers.

My thanks also go to Susan Turbié who has spent precious hours going through and improving every sentence of this book. Yannick Leroux and Esther Jacobs have also contributed significantly to the book with their meticulous revisions and additions, for which I thank them warmly.

Thanks also to Lisa Bucher, who kept the tempo of the final stages of the finished book. By this, I mean the illustrations, the design, the different stages of publication and all aspects related to the communication and promotion of the book. Thank you for refusing each of my attempts to negotiate deadlines.

To Jordy Den Hollander who initially lit the design spark of this great journey, your input was as always, truly appreciated.

My longtime friend Yannick Leroux and I studied together, then we were colleagues and now we are co-founders. Without him, Black Winch would still be just a one-man show.

I would like to thank Philip Blauw, founder of INNAX, for believing in the Black Winch project and for regularly challenging the model before it was even launched, with innocuous but always well-placed phrases in our conversations around good French wines.

Erik Swart, Country Leader Enterprise Apple, shares the same vision of As-A-Service, from technology devices to his jacuzzi. He encouraged me deeply to make it a business and even a lifestyle.

It was Baptiste Jourdan, co-founder of Toucan Toco, who invited me into the entrepreneurial journey. He shared with me his business drive and eye for opportunities.

Without being able to mention them all, I would like to acknowledge all my former colleagues from the Econocom and ECS groups with whom I developed the skills that today allow me to broaden the scope of As-A-Service to areas beyond IT.

I would like to express my thanks to you, clients and friends of Black Winch. Thank you for having dared to try As-A-Service with us and for having trusted us all along the way.

Finally, I thank my children, Félix and Julie, who accept the fact that I live "As-A-Service", breaking codes, and unfortunately making our quality time more rare but certainly more intense when we travel together. I am grateful to their mother, Ilse, who also makes this possible by taking care of them when I am not around.

Yann Toutant

Follow the authors
As-A-Service life
on instagram

Order this book
for a friend or leave
a review on Amazon

Engage
with the author
on LinkedIn

Colophon

© 2022 Yann Toutant – www.blackwinch.eu

ISBN 979 88 136 7335 1

Design
Cover design by Jordy den Hollander - jordy.denhollander@outlook.com
and Bert Holtkamp - mail@bertholtkamp.nl
Interior design by Bert Holtkamp - mail@bertholtkamp.nl
Illustrations by Veronika Zhdanko - zhdanko.veronika98@gmail.com

Editing
Coaching and developmental editing by Esther Jacobs –
www.estherjacobs.info
Language and editing by Susan Turbié - suse_paris@hotmail.fr
Second editing by Hugh Barker - https://reedsy.com/
Third editing by Laura Matthews - Synergyvaservice@gmail

Made in the USA
Middletown, DE
09 May 2024

54102184R00093